Mediterranean Diet for Beginners

A Complete Guide and Mediterranean Diet Cookbook with 14 Day Diet Meal Plan

By Junia Watt

Table of Contents

Breakfast Wrap
Mediterranean Scramble
Mediterranean Egg Salad

Lunch

Humble Oatmeal
Cod and Shrimp Soup
Red Pepper Pasta
Bean Salad
Stuffed Grape Leaves
Chicken and Couscous Burrito
Feta and Couscous Wrap
Tuna Salad
Creamy Chicken Pita
Whole Wheat Avocado and Cheese Sandwich
Chickpea and Pepper Salad
Buffet Bento
Hummus and Chickpea Pita
Tomato and Avocado Salad
Falafel Bowls
Lettuce Wraps

Dinner

Greek Meatballs
Mediterranean Potato and Zucchini Bake
Roasted Red Mullet Tomato Salad
Stuffed Pepper and Quinoa
Ras-el-honout Baked Chicken
Eggplant Rolls with Salad
Chicken Bake
Roasted Lamb and Veggies
Chicken with Prunes and Rice
Harissa Baked Cod and Bulgar
Red Pepper Chicken and Quinoa
Salmon and Beet with Rice
Cannellini Bean Stew
Lemon-Garlic Shrimp
Roasted Mediterranean Chicken
Shrimp Piccata with Zoodles

Desserts

Evoo Cake
Figs and Cheese
Avocado and Blueberry Bang
Date Truffles
Chocolate Mousse
Banana Strawberry Smoothie
Dried Figs with Walnuts and Ricotta
Summer Fruit Granita
Strawberry and Ricotta Parfait
Honey Pistachio Pears
Chia Seed Pumpkin Pudding
Halva
Roasted Figs and Spicy Mascarpone
Greek Parfait
Italian Apple Olive Oil Cake
Chocolate Chip Cookies
Brownies
Greek Yogurt Chocolate Mousse
Turkish Yogurt Cake with Figs

Snacks

Calamari Rings
Peanut Butter Popcorn
Parmesan Herbed Walnuts
Eggplant Crunchy Bites
Pita Pizza
Feta Triangle
Halloumi Sticks
Feta Dip
Cinnamon Couscous
Panzanella
Crunchy Chickpeas
Hummus
Pita Chips
Greek Nachos
Trail Mix
Smoked Salmon Bites

Conclusion

Introduction

Congratulations on getting *Mediterranean Diet for Beginners* and thank you for doing so.

There are many things that a person can love about the Mediterranean diet. It is full of healthy whole foods and is easy to implement into your life. It is one of the healthiest diets. Your body is nourished and balanced so that it functions its best.

When the diet you follow makes you feel like you are on vacation, why wouldn't you want to follow it? It is very likely that once you finish reading this book, you will start to find foods on your dinner table that fit into a Mediterranean diet. That said, like with any diet, you should check with your physician to make sure that it is safe for you. This isn't a diet for everyone.

When following any diet, the goal is to become healthier. I want to share with you the transformative power of this diet. There are a lot of positive changes that people have experienced while following the Mediterranean diet.

If you already know about the Mediterranean diet, then you can enjoy all of the recipes that are in this book. If you aren't familiar with it, you will be once you finish this book. And in both cases, you will have plenty of delicious meals to enjoy for a long time.

There are plenty of books on this subject on the market, so thanks again for choosing this one! Every effort was made to ensure it is full of as much useful information as possible. Please enjoy!

Chapter 1: What is the Mediterranean Diet

The Mediterranean diet isn't just a diet — it is a lifestyle. It is a way to eat so you can live a healthier and fuller life. When you follow this lifestyle, you will lose weight, but you are also going to strengthen your heart and give your body all the nutrients it needs in order to live longer and be more productive. People who follow the Mediterranean diet have been linked with lower risks of cancer, stroke, type 2 diabetes, Alzheimer's disease, better heart health, along with a longer lifespan. The building blocks to the Mediterranean diet are fresh fruits, vegetables, low saturated fats, and foods that are rich in healthy oils.

This diet focuses on normal recipes and foods that you would find in the cooking styles of the Mediterranean people. Here is what you can expect to eat during this diet. You will be eating a lot of pasta, rice, fruits, grains, and vegetables. You will limit fats, replace salt with spices and herbs and exchange red meat with poultry. The Mediterranean diet doesn't use much red meat. Nuts are eaten as a snack if needed, but you need to limit it to just a handful per day. Nuts do have a high-fat content, but it isn't saturated fats. Nuts also contain a lot of calories, so you have to carefully monitor what you eat. You need to stay away from candied, honey-roasted, and salted nuts.

You could even have a glass of red wine each day. Regular physical activity is needed to maximize all the wonderful health benefits. The Mediterranean diet includes many different eating habits of the communities in the countries around and near the Mediterranean Sea during the 1930s to the 1960s. These countries include Spain, France, Morocco, Greece, and Southern Italy. Because of this locality, the climate supports fresh vegetables, fruits, and the best varieties of seafood in the world.

These communities along the Mediterranean Sea have a very low risk of developing diseases when compared to Americans. Many studies have been performed and shown that this diet is great for our wellbeing and health.

This diet doesn't cut out fats altogether. It just helps you focus on the right types of fats. This diet doesn't allow you to eat saturated and trans fats which are linked with heart disease.

The grains that are used in the Mediterranean diet are whole grains and contain little unhealthy trans-fat. Bread is very important to this lifestyle. It just shouldn't be covered in butter or margarine. The bread can be eaten plain or dipped in olive oil. This will cut down tremendously on the number of saturated and trans fats that go along with eating bread.

Wine also has a large role in the Mediterranean diet. A glass of wine is usually included during the evening meal. This doesn't mean you get to drink a whole bottle of wine. You would be consuming five ounces or less if you are over 65 years old and ten ounces or less if you are younger than 65. If you are a recovering alcoholic, you shouldn't drink the wine at all. This also goes for anyone who has a heart or liver disease.

Olive oil is the main source of fat in this diet. It gives you monounsaturated fat which helps reduce your LDL cholesterol levels. Virgin and extra virgin olive oils haven't gone through all the processing that most oils do. They also contain the biggest levels of protective plant compounds that are responsible for giving antioxidants.

Fatty fish is another large component of the Mediterranean lifestyle. This will include albacore tuna, mackerel, herring, sardines, salmon, and lake trout. These are loaded with omega 3 fatty acids that help to decrease triglyceride levels and decrease blood clotting. Having a high triglyceride level of more than 150 mg per DL could contribute to heart disease. Omega 3 fatty acids can help to lower blood pressure, decrease the risk of heart attacks, and improve the health of blood vessels.

Most people wonder how often they can eat specific foods. With this new lifestyle, you can enjoy foods such as fruits, beans, whole grains, vegetables, cheese, and yogurt every day. Foods like meat, eggs, and fish need to be consumed once or twice per week. You will soon realize that this will be easier than it sounds once you have adjusted to this new way of eating.

The Mediterranean diet contains around 35 to 40 percent fats. Remember, it focuses mostly on the healthy fats. Even though they are higher in calories, these will make your food taste better and your meals more satisfying. You will eat less but will enjoy your food a lot more.

Many people have asked if they are going to feel hungry when following this diet. This answer is an easy "No." Because the Mediterranean diet puts an emphasis on high fiber foods such as whole grains, legumes, fresh fruits, beans, and vegetables, you shouldn't ever have any large hunger pangs as you do with other diets out there. You might be eating less, but your stomach isn't going to feel like it is.

This lifestyle plays a huge role in supporting your diet plan. You will want to get a lot of exercises but still have time to enjoy your meals with friends and family.

The great thing about this diet is it doesn't require you to purchase any specialty foods. This means that you won't be wasting money on buying foods that are labeled as diet or low fat. There are some exceptions. This diet consists of more natural foods and less processed foods. The more natural foods that you can incorporate into your diet daily, the better you are going to be.

You have to make a huge commitment before deciding to undergo this new lifestyle. You are going to spend more time in the kitchen preparing your meals because natural foods aren't easy to just grab and go. Learning to cook all these natural whole foods can be a challenge at first.

If you can plan out weekly meals on one day, do your shopping on another, and then prep your meals on the weekend, it will make this process a lot easier. It will also make sure you have healthy meals on hand if you don't feel like cooking.

Just like all other diets, it is extremely important to stay hydrated. Try to drink no less than 64 ounces of water every day. If your muscles begin to cramp or you get headaches, drink more water.

It might help to keep a log of your meals. When you keep track of what you eat, it can help you stay motivated and on track.

The Mediterranean Diet is made up of the following:

- Popular spices like mint, rosemary, lemon, oregano, basil, and garlic will be used to replace salt.
- Whole grain bread and pasta can be eaten without margarine or butter.
- Olive oil is the main source of fat. Margarine and butter aren't allowed.
- Red meat is eaten in smaller portions, limiting the intake to just a few times each month.
- You can have a glass of wine with your evening meal.
- Eat some type of fish twice weekly.
- Fresh fruits and vegetables are a part of each meal.
- Eat moderately sized cheese or yogurt each day.
- Moderately eating eggs and poultry just once a week.
- Drink 64 ounces of water daily.

A Very Healthy Diet

Many have claimed that the Mediterranean diet is the healthiest one in the entire world. This is due to the types of foods that are consumed. You will eat fish, seafood, legumes, olive oil, fruits, vegetables, and whole grains. Red meat isn't eaten more than maybe once every two weeks.

This diet focuses on recipes and foods of the Mediterranean. This isn't your normal diet — it is more of a lifestyle change. Just think of it as a new way to live and eat. When you follow this lifestyle, you can make well-balanced choices that will boost your health. The food tastes great and promotes the development of lean muscle mass and weight loss.

While following this new lifestyle, you need to stay away from the unhealthy ingredients and foods listed below. Just to be safe, be sure you read all food labels well to see and stay away from these foods:

- High processed foods: This includes any foods that are labeled as low fat or diet or any that have been processed in a factory.

- Trans fats: Be sure you find substitutes for margarine and butter.

- Refined grains: These will include white bread and any pasta that has been made from refined grains.

- Processed meats: These will include hot dogs, sausages, ham, etc.

- Refined oils: These will include canola, cottonseed, and soybean oils.

- Added sugars: Stay away from table sugar, sodas, candies, and ice cream.

History

The Mediterranean basin has more than 22 countries in Asia, Africa, and Europe. The people in the communities around this basin eat mainly plant foods such as vegetables, fruits, olive oil, nuts, seeds, legumes, and whole grains. There are just a few regional variations of this diet, and these don't even change the diet due to so many similarities. This diet's origins reflect the diverse population and intricate interactions of the people who lived there over several centuries.

The people's diet that lived in France, Italy, Greece, Spain, and Morocco were thought of as the poor man's diet. This diet was developed over several thousands of years. These inhabitants worked to produce food in very poor terrain.

The plants that grew there consisted of capers, olive trees, and grapevines. Capers have a very intense flavor. The olive tree is symbolic of all the plants that grow in the region. It is very significant to the biggest religions in the Mediterranean, which are Judaism, Islam, and Christianity.

Most of the local dishes were influenced by a history of various ethnic cultures from Arabian to Spanish to Italian. This region has been a crossroad for civilizations and a center for culture. The region was occupied by Phoenicians, Romans, and Carthaginians by 3000 B.C.

- Traditional Dishes

Meals during this time were influenced by what foods were available and culture. Many of the dishes consisted of tomatoes, eggplant, potatoes, and seafood. They flavored their foods with spices that came from North Africa. Families would go to their garden to figure out what they were going to eat for dinner. Their dishes were very simple. Their dinners included local ingredients since importing foods from other countries were expensive. Sugar was very expensive to import, so they would use honey and other natural sweeteners, too.

Even though there was a lot of seafood and fish in their diets, the residents on the coast of the Mediterranean were mainly farmers instead of fishermen. Iconic dishes like pesto was very common. This was made from garlic, basil, olive oil, and raw tomatoes. A different iconic dish was fish couscous. It consisted of a variety of legumes, seafood, and vegetables. Pantescan salad was made with capers, potatoes, tomatoes, and red onions.

The caponata was another popular dish that was made with olive oil, eggplant, and capers. All of these dishes were common around the Mediterranean. Each region would have small differences. All of these local foods were hearty, rich, and full of flavor. These were flavored with capers, olive oil, and wild herbs.

Public Acknowledgement

This diet was publicly announced by Ancel Keys, who was an American biologist, along with the help of his wife, Margaret, who was a chemist, in the 1960s. It didn't gain public recognition until the early 1990s. Studies from Naples and Madrid were the first information sources on the benefits and usefulness of this amazing diet.

Studies have been done across the seven countries along the Mediterranean and were published in the 1970s. One report that was released in the 1980s followed these studies very closely. Walter Willett who worked at Harvard University's School of Public Health was given credit for being the first to produce an accepted version of this diet. He released the publication in the middle of the 1990s.

- High Amounts of Fats

Researchers were amazed by the huge amounts of fats the occupants of the communities around the Mediterranean ate. This is the main reason why many people thought it was just a paradox. It contradicted the fact that these people ate very high amounts of fat but had the lowest rates of cardiovascular and heart disease as compared to people who lived in America.

At that time, people were amazed at this puzzle because there were no signs of heart disease. In countries like England, their residents ate a lot of fat but were nowhere as healthy as the Mediterranean's. This is called the French Paradox.

French Paradox

This is just a catchphrase that was used in the 1980s. It refers to the paradox that was based on mere observation. The citizens of France had low levels of cardiovascular and heart problems in spite of eating a diet that was rich in saturated fats.

This contrasted greatly to the acceptance of the time that normal consumption of foods that are high in saturated fats created a risk for cardiovascular and coronary heart disease. The puzzle comes from the fact that if science links saturated fats to heart disease held true, then the people of France should have high levels of heart disease when compared to countries where diets are low in saturated fats.

Two possibilities are implied with the French Paradox. One is there is a link between saturated fats and heart disease, but the diet and lifestyle of the French diminish against the risk. If they could identify the factor, then it might explain this puzzle. Another possibility is there isn't any valid hypothesis that links heart disease to saturated fats.

If the factor that diminishes the paradox is identified, then it could be applied to lifestyles and diets of other countries. This might save lives so people can be just as healthy as the French.

French Diet

Over the years, it has been realized that the diet of French people who lack trans fats is rich in short-chain saturated fatty acids. One researcher, Frank Cooper, noted that the French Paradox exists because there aren't any hydrogenated and trans fats in the French diet.

There is a very large difference between the American and French diets. American's eat mainly large amounts of hydrogenated vegetable oil whereas the French eat natural saturated fats like those found in cream, nuts, and cheese.

These are simple for our bodies to digest and metabolize. The American diet that is full of hydrogenated fats is hard to metabolize and cause certain health risks.

Comparing the Mediterranean and French Diet

- They focus on pleasure, variety, freshness, and balance.

- People from the Mediterranean area always sit and eat their meals. They savor every mouthful.

- They only eat three meals each day. They don't snack during the day.

- They eat small quantities of food that is high quality when compared to Americans who eat huge amounts of low-quality foods.

- They drink a lot of herbal teas, soups, and water.

- The people of the Mediterranean eat less between meals. They stay away from unhealthy options such as processed foods, deep fried foods, snacks, and sodas.

- They eat a lot of foods with full fat but aren't full of sugar. They have a very low sugar intake. Americans eat huge amounts of sugar indirectly and directly. Most of the low fat and no fat foods have huge amounts of sugar.

- Mediterranean people get about 80 percent of their fats from dairy and vegetable sources like whole milk yogurt, whole milk, and cheese. This proves that the diet consists of good fats. Americans usually eat unhealthy hydrogenated fats.

- They eat small portions and divide meals into courses. This lets the food they eat to digest before they add more food to their stomach.

- People from the Mediterranean region consume more fish as compared to Americans. Fish contain healthy oil that is rich in Omega 2 fatty acids.

Aspects of the Diet

1. Nutrition during the early years: A good reason why this diet is superior to the American diet is that of the dietary improvements during a child's early years. These improvements go to the children throughout every generation. Some governments make an effort to introduce nutrition programs that give quality foods and nutrition to pregnant women and young children in order to make them healthier. This nutrition can explain

the low levels of obesity and heart disease across countries that border the Mediterranean Sea.

2. More fruits and vegetables: It is now evident that eating more fruits and vegetables will reduce the chances of developing cardiovascular diseases.

3. Whole Diet: Scientists have found that there isn't one nutrient that makes this diet beneficial but a combination of nutrients that are in whole foods like nuts, vegetables, and fruits, etc. This diet doesn't focus on a certain amount of fats or proteins that get eaten, but the whole content of nutrients that are in a meal made with natural foods. The focus is never on processed foods, only whole natural foods.

Mediterranean Diet in Portugal

Researchers who have studied this diet compared it to the diet of Americans and other developed countries. During this study, they referred to the Mediterranean diet as a poor man's diet. They also viewed Portugal's diet was the purest form of this diet. The main problem was back in the 60s and 70s, Portugal's dictator didn't want his country to be associated with this diet.

The Portuguese call their diet the "Atlantic Diet." This is the Mediterranean diet but with more leafy greens, fish, and other seafood.

Scientific Principle

The main problem with most Western diets is the problem of heart disease, which has increased in the past century. During the 1970s, the dietary intake of sugary foods and excessive carbs increased greatly. This made scientists try to figure out why people who lived in the Mediterranean region had such extremely low rates of this disease. During the 1980s, their main study was called MONICA or "Multinational Monitoring of Trends and Determinants in Cardiovascular Disease." They collected ten years' worth of data, and it looked at 21 different countries. The results were astonishing, and they became the foundation of the belief that this is, in fact, was the best diet around. One other study done in 2003 asked 772 volunteers and tested them for three months. Once again, the results showed a huge decrease in blood pressure and blood sugar levels for the ones who followed the Mediterranean diet as opposed to those who did a low-fat diet. Other studies have shown that increasing the consumption of nuts within five years can reduce the risk of death caused by a cardiovascular event by up to 63 percent. For people who cook with olive oil daily have a lower mortality rate than those who cook with regular vegetable oil. This is just one more reason to change to the Mediterranean diet.

Chapter 2: Living Healthier with the Mediterranean Diet

With findings that show a 30 percent reduction in heart disease, we need to take these studies seriously. Isn't that enough to encourage you to change how you eat? What about the studies that showed Mediterranean foods could stop the brain from shrinking as we age, which has been connected to consuming foods that are plant-based?

The Mediterranean diet is said to be the best lifestyle and diet in the world. This diet has been proven to be helpful in many ways. This is due to the emphasis on fresh produce, fish, healthy fats, antioxidants, high fiber intake, whole grains, along with a moderate intake of alcohol and red meat.

When you follow this lifestyle, you will enjoy your meals with loved ones since you will be preparing the majority of your meals at home. Cooking as a family and relaxing with a glass of red wine afterward is the kind of life many Mediterranean people enjoy. This diet requires you to eat a lot of fresh produce. You should try to eat five small meals during the day that include healthy oils along with fresh fruit and vegetables. These oils could be from olive oil, nuts, fish, or avocado. Each meal should include some of the following: cheese, yogurt, eggs, and fish.

You won't find any foods that are salt or sugar processed or that are high in saturated fats. These foods cause people to develop cardiovascular disease.

This diet is thought of as the ideal diet since you don't have to go to extremes with it. You will be able to enjoy a wonderful quality of life while enjoying delicious foods that you and your family will enjoy. You get to eat regularly without skipping any meals. When you begin this lifestyle, you will notice a big difference in your life. You should expect to see a difference with your longevity, heart health, and brain.

Here is a list of benefits you can expect while following the Mediterranean diet:

1. *Keeps you agile as you age*

The meals you eat while following the Mediterranean diet contains many useful essential oils, vitamins, minerals, and many other nutrients. Since you are consuming all these nutrients, you should expect benefits in many different ways. You will have less risk of conditions like muscle weakness and fragility.

Senior citizens who follow this diet have shown great improvement in health with more muscle mass and stronger bones. The risk of these conditions could be reduced by 70 percent just by switching to this diet. If you would like to lead a successful lifestyle in your later years, start eating healthy fats, lean proteins, fruits, and vegetables. These help to keep your muscles lean and supple while keeping your body agile and your bones strong.

Mediterranean cuisine has been called the healthiest in the world, and this lifestyle doesn't stray from it. Since it is based mainly on seafood, poultry, whole grains, healthy oil, and fresh fruits and vegetables, it is easy to see why this diet is called healthy. Add in a glass of red wine and you have a fun and easy lifestyle.

2. *Healthy Heart*

Coronary and heart problems are a lot lower in the Mediterranean regions than in America and other parts of the world. This could be caused by diet choices of the people living in the Mediterranean region. Experts agree that the oils you get from olives, salmon, and nuts are heart healthy. They promote circulation and heart health.

Good dietary choices can enhance your heart health. Remember that it isn't what you eat that matters but what you drink. A glass of wine daily and lots of water supports a healthy heart and body. Red wine can lower the risk of heart disease. Remember to limit your intake to around ten ounces daily. This diet also promotes a very active lifestyle. It encourages social support and physical activity.

Moderation is the key to having a healthy body. The main aspect to focus on is bad cholesterol. This diet promotes healthy oils that are wonderful for the heart. It can help get rid of bad cholesterol that gets deposited in the arteries that can cause cardiovascular problems.

Evidence links heart health with specific foods like nuts, olive oil, fruits, and veggies. This diet has all that and then some.

This diet is about highlighting healthy fats. Stop using the normal cooking oil and use olive oil that contains healthy fats that are good for your heart. This being said, this diet could decrease the risk of heart failure. This lifestyle contains foods that have monounsaturated fats such as olive oil instead of saturated fats such as butter. The Mediterranean diet includes many of the main diet changes that keep your heart in the best shape possible.

3. *Protects against type 2 Diabetes*

Type 2 diabetes happens when there is too much-unregulated sugar in the blood. This is sometimes caused by consuming overly-processed starches and carbs that are high on the glycemic index. This diet has been proven to be more effective than any other diet when protecting against diabetes.

Scientists compared the Mediterranean diet with all other diets including high fiber, high protein, vegetarian, vegan, and many other diets. The results conclusively showed the Mediterranean diet was more effective at keeping diabetes at bay than any of the others. Scientists place emphasis on foods that contain monounsaturated oils like fruits, vegetables, salmon, and olive oil. It has been proven to lower blood sugar levels and cholesterol in people who have been diagnosed with diabetes.

Since this diet focuses on fresh ingredients and it contains many minerals, antioxidants, and vitamins, it is a great way to keep diabetes under control. This type of lifestyle will control excess insulin which will lower your blood sugar levels.

Keeping your blood sugar levels regulated is very important to living a healthy lifestyle. You have to find balance with whole foods to find quality sources of protein and carbs that are very low in sugar. This will make the body burn fat more and this will give you more energy. Basically, any diet made up of fresh produce will naturally combat diabetes.

4. Reduces the risk of Alzheimer's disease

With the Mediterranean diet, you get to eat foods that improve your blood sugar and lower cholesterol levels. It also improves the health of your cardiovascular system. These benefits will work together to help reduce your risk of developing Alzheimer's.

There is evidence that suggests this diet helps to protect against cognitive decline. By doing this, seniors can limit the burden of illness. It can help to maintain and preserve their quality of life. Doctors have advised patients to participate in healthier lifestyles like following the Mediterranean diet. Having healthy eating habits, staying busy during the day, and getting regular exercise can help with conditions such as dementia and other cognitive conditions.

5. A healthy way to lose weight

Many obese and overweight people struggle to lose weight. This is because they try to do things the wrong way. Most people try to do diets that are either temporary or they just don't work. It's important to change your lifestyle totally so you can enjoy all the benefits that come with your chosen lifestyle.

The main focus on the Mediterranean diet isn't to lose weight, but it can help with that if it is what you are looking for. Think about this for a minute: clean, fresh food along with less sugar, good fats, whole grains with lots of water, and exercise. When you transition your body to healthy foods along with a healthy lifestyle, you are going to shed some pounds without creating any drastic imbalances in your body. Plant-based diets are great to help people lose weight. The fact that you have stopped eating processed foods and junk foods that are loaded with unhealthy fats and sugars is a great way to lose weight.

Losing weight with the Mediterranean diet comes in various forms. None of the foods you will be eating are fattening. Every carb you eat is low on the glycemic index. This means they get digested slowly and will keep you feeling fuller for longer. They don't have any processed starches or carbs or oils that are unhealthy.

In order to lose a lot of weight healthily, you need to get active. You need to engage in exercise regularly. You could also take steps to be active like taking the stairs instead of the elevator or if it is close enough to you, walk to the grocery store. Keep your portions small at each meal. Don't overeat since this is the main reason behind obesity.

6. *Can fight cancer*

Scientists have found that the Mediterranean diet can fight cancer. Eating properly on this diet can lead to a reduced risk of cancer and deaths related to cancer. The main foods that contribute to the Mediterranean diet are salmon, fresh produce, olive oil, and other nutrients like omega 3 fatty acids, antioxidants, selenium, and trace elements and many others.

All of these nutrients will work to get rid of toxins in the body and gets rid of waste from the cells. Antioxidants can combat free radicals that are thought to be the beginning of cancer. Mediterranean diet also plays a huge role in preventing cancer. This lifestyle helps to prevent radical cancers from developing like breast cancer in postmenopausal women.

7. *Enhances relaxation*

This diet, surprisingly, encourages relaxation. It can lower insulin levels and can make you feel at ease. Having high blood sugar can cause you to become hyperactive and then crash later. Eating a balanced meal that includes vegetables, fruits, whole grains, and more can help to stabilize blood sugar, and this allows you to rest and relax.

When you decide to change to the Mediterranean lifestyle, you need to adopt other aspects to completely benefit from the lifestyle. This would mean you need to spend more time with family, cooking, and having meals together along with other activities, too. When you spend time with people you love, it will help to relax the mind and help release feel-good hormones.

Hormones like serotonin can help calm you down and help relax you. Keeping your heart and nerves calm can enhance your overall health and promotes your longevity. Eating delicious and nutritious meals while relaxing your body and mind will give you a relaxed life.

8. *Fights inflammation in the body*

Inflammation happens in the body. When it does happen, you are at risk of developing many major illnesses and this could compromise your health. There is good news in that the Mediterranean diet can help reduce inflammation. Studies have shown that a reduction in inflammation markers in people who are at high risk.

Inflammation can be caused by exposure to oxidative stress. The antioxidants that come from the food you eat while following the Mediterranean diet can combat oxidative stress very successfully. You can improve this by eating foods that contain choline like beetroots, spinach, and soybeans.

9. *Good for your skin*

Your skin is a critical organ that serves many purposes such as protecting your other organs and getting rid of waste. If you eat a lot of fruits and vegetables and foods that are rich in antioxidants, water, and olive oil, then you are going to love how your skin looks.

Omega 3 fatty acids are found in fish. They can strengthen the skin's membrane to help make it firmer and more elastic. Tomatoes, red wine, and olive oil contain antioxidants that protect the skin against damage that is done by prolonged sun exposure and chemical reactions.

10. *Cuts your chances in half for developing Parkinson's disease*

This debilitating disease will affect your quality of life in your later years. The Mediterranean diet gives you a lot of antioxidants. The number of antioxidants you eat in this diet cuts your risk in half. These can be found in the fruits, vegetables, seafood, and healthy fats.

These antioxidants help to protect your cells from being exposed to oxidative stress. Oxidative stress can damage cells and this can result in developing diseases such as Parkinson's.

11. Protects Cognitive Health

This wonderful diet can improve cognitive ability. Scientists have shown that people who follow this lifestyle have better attention and focus along with better memory. This diet can enhance the brain's capabilities. This is great for people who want to keep their brain function throughout their life. It can also fend off dementia in older people. You could experience a better quality of life as you age.

12. Improves mood

This new lifestyle gives a lot of benefits that help the brain. People who have challenges like anxiety, depression, and ADHD will get many benefits from the Mediterranean diet.

The issues happen because of a dopamine deficiency. Dopamine is a neurotransmitter that is responsible for regulating moods. Following this lifestyle on a regular basis can help your body make this chemical and helps keep your mood elevated and brain happy.

This diet could help you be more positive even if things aren't going well. Healthy living can do that. When you eat enough food that fills you with nutrients, your body is going to recognize that. Productivity and fulfillment can enhance your mood. Following the diet correctly is going to make it feel like you are treating yourself well and will enhance your mood.

13. Pain relief

Fiber-rich foods and whole grains are common with the Mediterranean diet. They are rich in magnesium and other nutrients. Leafy green vegetables and fresh fruits could help with pain management. This diet can help reduce your dependence on painkillers. Your body is going to respond to pain differently since this diet can combat inflammation and can help reduce stress levels. It is possible that your chronic pain might just disappear due to the Mediterranean diet.

14. Very affordable

This diet is completely doable even if you are on a tight budget. Olive oil, whole grains, herbs, fruits, vegetables, and legumes aren't as expensive as it seems, and they give you a lot of versatility when you are in the kitchen.

15. Boosts your brain power

This diet can counteract the brain's ability to perform. Choosing this lifestyle will help you preserve memory and this can lead to an increase in your cognitive health.

Cognitive disorders happen when your brain can't get the right amount of dopamine. It is responsible for sending information from neuron to neuron. It is responsible for proper body movements, mood regulation, and thought processing.

The Mediterranean diet's ability to boost cognitive health is linked to a combination of healthy nuts and fats and all the anti-inflammatory vegetables and fruits. These foods can battle cognitive decline that happens with age. How can these foods do this? These foods deal with things that create inflammation, toxicity, and free radicals that impair brain functions. Olive oil, nuts, and fatty fish contain omega 3 fatty acids that can help reduce inflammation in the body. Vegetables such as broccoli, kale, and spinach or any dark green vegetables contain vitamin E that protects the body from anti-inflammatory molecules called cytokines.

Vegetables such as watermelon, cherries, raspberries, broccoli, and spinach have antioxidants that will neutralize free radicals that can affect the brain. This diet focuses on monounsaturated fats that come from olive oil. The fatty acids and oils you get from omega 3 fatty acids combine to keep your arteries clear. This will automatically increase your brain's health.

Be Intelligent About the Diet

If you don't monitor your diet closely, you could suffer from some of these side effects. Luckily, there are ways to prevent these from becoming major issues.

1. You could begin to gain weight if you don't watch the amount of olive oil and nuts you eat. These are extremely high in fat, so you have to watch how many you are eating every day.

2. You might have some calcium loss from not eating as much dairy. If this happens, start taking a calcium supplement.

3. Your iron levels might become low. Make sure you eat more foods that are rich in iron or vitamin C.

If you are a recovering alcoholic, it might be best if you didn't incorporate the red wine into your diet. The main idea is to get healthier and not to endanger yourself. These side effects are fairly small in comparison to other diets. These side effects can be easily reversed with some time and attention.

During the first few weeks of the diet, your body will adjust and purge itself of all the toxins that were built up in the body. During this time, you might feel bad. This is totally normal. When your body has gotten rid of all the sugars and toxins in your body, you are going to notice more energy and an improvement in your well-being.

Chapter 3: Starting the Mediterranean Diet

As we have established, the Mediterranean diet's origins go back to the basin of the Mediterranean Sea. Many scientists consider this region as the cradle of society. This is due to the fact that the ancient world's history took place at this very spot. Civilizations like the Egyptians lived across the Mediterranean Sea along the Nile River.

According to UNESCO, they define the Mediterranean diet as a social practice, way of life, and lifestyle. This involves traditions and knowledge that ranges from cooking food, preparing that food, fishing, processing, harvesting, conservation, and cultures in specific ways.

Food Model

This diet has been called a food model. It enhances the quality and safety of food along with links to the land. Meals offer basic cuisines that are rich in nutrition, flavors, and taste. It takes advantage of every aspect of what the people there consider to be a very healthy diet. This diet is a choice that keeps all the traditions and customs of the inhabitants along the Mediterranean Sea.

Eating this diet regularly is very nourishing. It can have a very profound effect on a person's health. Good nutrition can help prevent diseases such as obesity, diabetes, and hypertension. This diet can affect the health of communities and individual families since good nutrition can prevent diseases and maintain levels of excellent health. Experts think this diet is useful because it enables development that is useful to all the countries that border the Mediterranean Sea and over the world along with the economic and cultural effects of the food.

Health, Flavors, and Colors

Many benefits are associated with this diet and all of them can be attributed to Ancel Keys who is an American scientist who works at the University of Minnesota. He identified the connection between cardiovascular diseases and the Mediterranean diet. His research came about because he wondered how the poor residents who lived along the Mediterranean Sea were so much healthier than the wealthy inhabitants in cities like London and New York.

He researched this for some time and figured out it had to do with what they ate and this is why he went on an expedition to learn about the Mediterranean diet. The results of this study concluded that this diet can actually lower cholesterol. Due to this, people from that region didn't suffer from coronary conditions or heart disease. The reasons behind this were their regular use of foods like red onions, herbs, garlic, bread, vegetables, olive oil, and pasta. All of the products were used of vegetable origin and they didn't use a lot of red meat.

This wasn't the only study that has been done by American scientists. Many other studies have been done about the health benefits of this diet. There were many overlapping agreements from all these studies. One was the complete recognition of the many beneficial qualities from living and eating this way. Many studies along with clinical studies have shown over and over again the many advantages and benefits of the Mediterranean diet. This is why many people think of it as more of a lifestyle instead of a diet.

Another benefit is its ability to reduce the size of a person's waist, lower blood pressure, reduce blood sugar, increase HDL, and reduce the number of triglycerides or dangerous fats. Please realize that this diet alone will not give you these amazing results. These benefits aren't going to be automatic. You have to take deliberate steps in order to enjoy these benefits. There are some risk factors that you might need to modify.

Some factors that might need to be modified is the correct intake of calories, stop smoking, getting physical activity. You have to also be able to control any metabolic disease like hypertension, diabetes, and obesity. Being able to manage your stress levels or living a stress-free life is recommended, too. Consuming a balanced diet and being disciplined in your lifestyle are also recommended.

Middle Ages

The traditions of the ancient Romans influenced the communities' diets that lived along the coast of the Mediterranean. Some foods that are associated with the influence of the Greeks and Romans include oil products, bread, and wine. These products were also symbols of their culture. The food options back then included vegetables such as leeks, chicory, mushrooms, mallow, lettuce, fish, seafood, cheese made from sheep's milk, along with a tiny amount of red meat.

In the regions of Germany, pig fat was used when cooking. The small amount of grain that they produced wasn't used for food but was fermented to make beer. This was introduced into the Mediterranean but wasn't accepted by its people. There was also Morocco and Arabs across the Mediterranean along with others. The Muslim and Arab regions created their own culture of food, which was very unique.

Many foods in this diet are borrowed from the influences of the Islamic communities who lived in the region. Muslims gave the region agriculture and they borrowed much of their food from it. Some food crops they cultivated were spinach, spices, sugar cane, citrus, rice, and eggplant. This cuisine involved products that came from Europe like pomegranates, rose water, orange, lemons, and almonds.

It isn't clear how foods from Europe couldn't influence the Mediterranean's diet, but North African and Muslim cultures did. Other foods were introduced into the diet later. This occurred when the Europeans thought they had discovered America. This opened another world of exotic foods. Some of these foods that came from the New World included beans, tomatoes, pepper, chili, and potatoes.

Cereal vs. Vegetable

Tomatoes were first thought of as an ornamental fruit but later became the first red fruit before it became the symbol of the Mediterranean. Even though the tomato is the most critical fruit of this diet, the role that is played by cereals shouldn't be overlooked.

Cereals provide the base for simple cooking along with being a tool for daily survival. Cereals help fill hungry stomachs and were seen as a weapon of survival especially for the poor. There are various kinds of cereals and they are prepared and consumed differently for various purposes. They were used as a base for paella, polenta, pasta, couscous, bread, and soup.

There are some similarities between the foods that are consumed by the people of the Mediterranean have been influenced by foods from our ancestors, the Muslims, and the new Americas.

Nutritious Diet

This diet is nutritious and has been appreciated and accepted universally. Eating this diet supports all the aspects of our health. It has been proven that eating has a profound effect on our health. This is because good nutrition can help you manage your health along with preventing diseases such as coronary heart conditions, diabetes, cancer, high blood pressure, and hypertension.

Nutritionists in America described the Mediterranean diet as pasta dishes and homemade minestrone with a dash of Parmesan, small fish, some red meat, macaroni, tomato sauce, and bread hot out of the oven. This diet includes fresh fruit to be eaten as dessert along with vegetables that get sprinkled with tasty olive oil.

Rich in Fiber

This diet contains many nutrients and is rich in unsaturated fats, fiber, and antioxidants. It can help reduce the consumption of animal fats and cholesterol.

Food Pyramid

There are a few concepts about the Food Pyramid. One of them is proportionality. This means we need to pick the correct amount of food from every food group. The other one is a portion that stands for the quantity of food that will be eaten.

There is also variety and this simply implies the opportunity to pick foods. On the bottom of the diet food pyramid is grains. There is a huge variety that you can choose from. This includes potatoes, grains, rice, bread, and pasta. Grains are followed by all sorts of fruits. Vegetables and fruits are an important aspect and get ranked in this way. Since there is so much to choose from, you can eat a different one each day.

After vegetables and fruits will be low-fat cheese, yogurt, olive oil, and legumes. These need to be consumed daily. Even though meat is included, it doesn't rank that high. There is a preference for poultry like turkey and chicken rather than beef. Beef is only consumed rarely like maybe one or two times each month.

The pyramid allows interchangeability. This basically means you have a huge variety of foods that you can choose from in every group. Variety is critical for keeping this lifestyle.

The Mediterranean diet gives amazing culture to people who live in the region of the Mediterranean and other parts of the world through their food. It gives a huge source of delicious and tasty foods and recipes. The people who live in the Mediterranean regions eat foods that they grow in their region.

Scientists and nutritionists agree that eating this diet regularly can give the body the nutrients it needs. This diet could even prevent several diseases especially the ones that are metabolic in nature. This diet is an excellent source of health for the body. It promotes longevity along with other benefits. It has found acceptance by medics and patients in American and all over the world.

What Does the Mediterranean Diet Change?

Your heart won't be the only thing that will thank you for following the Mediterranean diet. There will be other changes to your body.

- Weight loss, as long as you watch your portion sizes and get regular exercise.

- Consuming healthy antioxidants helps to reduce the effects of shrinkage of the brain as you age. This will reduce the risk of developing Alzheimer's and Parkinson's disease.

- Vitamin E improves the skin's glow and condition.

- Lowers blood sugar levels. This is great for people who have type 2 diabetes.

- Produces high rates of dopamine within the brain. This can lead to improved moods and feelings of wellbeing.

- Strengthens bones and muscles. Studies show an increase of 70 percent in elderly people who consume the Mediterranean diet.

- Helps to fight inflammation.

- Reduces the risk of developing cancer cells.

- Reduces the chance of developing neurological diseases.

- Increases better concentration skills and energy levels.

Combine the Mediterranean Diet with Exercise

If you want to lose weight, exercising each day will speed up this process. A brisk walk twice a week that will take you about an hour is an ideal way to start. You could also do 30-minute exercises like swimming, bike riding, or walking four times each week. You could even invent a home workout. This is just a minimum guideline. The amount of exercise you decide to do on top of this depends on the amount of time you have for exercise.

Exercising alone doesn't guarantee you are going to lose weight. What you could do is increase your calorie intake by an extra 200 calories on the days that you exercise. You are already doing your heart a big favor by eating a heart-friendly diet. If you combine that with basic exercises, you are going to have more energy along with a healthy body. Exercise along with the Mediterranean diet can help you keep your body healthy and help you lose some weight.

Tricks and Tips for Success

If you want to apply the Mediterranean diet to your life in order to lose weight, these diet tips along with the eating habits of the Mediterranean diet will help maximize weight loss.

1. Have a well-balanced plan

The longer you can stick with the Mediterranean diet, the more vitality and energy you will have.

This diet has a well-balanced eating plan that tells you the correct amount of food you should eat in each of the food groups.

2. Eat slowly

It generally takes about 20 minutes for your food to begin digesting before it starts making you feel full after you have eaten. This means you should slow down and chew slowly, so you are actually tasting the food and enjoying its flavor. If you eat fast, you may realize that you eat more since it takes 20 minutes to get your stomach ready to digest food.

3. Change up saturated fats for monounsaturated fats

Give your weight loss a supercharge by replacing your saturated fats for monounsaturated fats. The Mediterranean diets change the normal bad fat with high levels of healthy fats that will raise your good cholesterol levels.

4. Drink water before you eat

Try to drink an eight-ounce glass of water before eating a meal. Thirst is sometimes mistaken for hunger. Drinking water before eating can jump-start the digestion process faster which could cause you to eat less.

5. Purchase smaller bowls and plates

When you fill a small bowl or plate, you will still feel satisfied because in your eyes, you had a full plate to eat. With smaller plates, you will still feel full because you are eating healthy portions that stick with the Mediterranean diet's food pyramid.

6. Divide your plate into three separate sections

Try to visually divide your plate in half and then divide a half in two. This gives you three sections. One large one and two small ones.

You will be putting your vegetables in the large section. The two small sections are for protein and starches. You can use this as a guide to measure when you eat out at a restaurant or if you just want to turn your dinner plate into healthy portions.

You are going to get the largest level of phytonutrients from veggies, so this is why vegetables take up the largest portion of the plate.

7. Get rid of cookies and cakes

If you tend to binge on cookies and cakes, try eating a serving of popcorn that was popped in olive oil. For an extra boost, sprinkle on some garlic powder and parmesan cheese instead of butter and salt.

8. Exercise

You need to make sure you do the lowest level on the Mediterranean pyramid. This is your daily activity. Try to get no less than 30 minutes of exercise each day.

9. Have a snack twice a day

With the Mediterranean diet, you can have a snack two to three times every day as long as you have a serving of fresh vegetables or fruits without adding sugar or salt. You could schedule a snack in the early afternoon, late afternoon, and before bed, if needed.

10. Change how you think about food

Look at fruits and vegetables as snack foods. Slice the veggies into ready to eat sizes and wash the fruits as soon as you bring them home so they are ready to grab for a quick snack when you feel hungry.

Have a container of mixed nuts within arm's length on the kitchen counter and have a handful with your fruit or vegetable snack.

Use olive oil instead of margarine and butter. Use olive oil when grilling sandwiches or toasting bread rather than using butter.

11. Prepackaged snacks

Package snacks into small portions size instead of eating from a full container. This helps you prevent overeating. When you allow how large your snack is, you are helping discipline yourself.

Chapter 4: Eating on the Mediterranean Diet

People think the Mediterranean diet might be the solution for anybody who wants to start living a sustainable and healthy lifestyle because of all the wonderful food groups you get to eat.

By now, you have seen that this diet is rich in seafood, fish, olive oil, seeds, nuts, whole grains, fruits, and vegetables. It is very low in red meats and totally free of refined foods and artificial sugars.

The Mediterranean diet gives you a chance for a new lifestyle instead of just another diet. If you decide to do this lifestyle, you are going to be eating whole foods with nutrients that are great for your body. You won't have to count carbs as most diets require you. You don't have to eat five meals daily.

You will instead have to eat real foods and get rid of all the processed foods. Evidence has proven that this diet is healthy for you. This evidence proves that this diet can give you a better quality of life and improve your health. Other improvements you might experience include reduced risk of illnesses and permanent weight loss.

Aside from all the healthy foods, this diet features wonderful flavors that are luxurious. The food isn't just tasty but very nourishing. This diet brings tasty foods that are flavorful but also nutritious and healthy.

This is the main reason experts love this lifestyle as one of the healthiest and best in the whole world. If you would like to eat foods that are beneficial for your wellbeing and health, then the following foods come highly recommended.

Replacing hydrogenated and saturated fats with olive oil is the biggest change you will have to make with the Mediterranean diet. Everything gets cooked in olive oil. This includes marinades and salad dressings. They do grow their own olives in the Mediterranean, so it isn't surprising why this oil is the most popular. Other healthy choices are avocados and olives. You are basically increasing your intake of plant-based foods. Never cook with butter if a recipe calls for olive oil. Never use salt to make foods "tastier," use spices and herbs. Red meat isn't completely off the menu, just eat it a few times per month. Lean white meat is better for you. Fish is another important ingredient that is included in this diet and should be eaten twice weekly.

The foundation of the diet is social and substantial. You need to eat with friends and family, dancing, participating in sports, and walking. People who live in hot climates do these activities. All of this plays a huge role in the Mediterranean lifestyle.

Here is a close look at foods that you should incorporate into the Mediterranean regularly:

1. Cauliflower

This is the most popular vegetable in this diet. It is extremely healthy and nourishes the body to keep it in wonderful health. It contains plant compounds that reduce the risk of diseases such as heart disease and cancer.

Cauliflower is used in many dishes and is useful due to its wonderful flavor and taste. It is full of nutrients and minerals that are good for your health. It's good for weight loss and is easy to add into your normal diet.

2. Almonds

Almonds are great for many reasons. First and foremost, they can help you lose weight for the long term. They taste great as a snack, milk, and nut butter. They are full of nutrients and healthy oils. They are high in fats but contain the good type of fat that is great for the heart. They are recommended since they are very healthy and nutritious.

If you exercise regularly, almonds could help you shed pounds faster. They make you feel fuller so you won't eat as much during meals.

Almonds are so healthy you can eat them any time of day. They are a high protein food but are loaded with heart-friendly fats. They also contain other nutrients like fiber, healthy fats, vitamin E, manganese, and magnesium. Almonds also contain trace elements of copper, vitamin B2, and phosphorus.

A handful of nuts can nourish your body and fill it with nutrients. You will get a lot of antioxidants since almonds are a great source. Almonds are full of vitamin E. Almonds are the best source of vitamin E in the world. Studies have linked low levels of heart disease with this powerful vitamin.

3. Hummus

Hummus is mostly used as a spread for bread or as a dip. You make it by blending spices, lemon juice, chickpeas, tahini, olive oil, and garlic. Chickpeas curb hunger and are full of plant protein. You can dip veggies in this tasty dip like celery and cucumber. Some popular ways to flavor this tasty spread is jalapeno, sage, black pepper, roasted red pepper, and sun-dried tomato. It is best if you make your own, but you could just buy hummus at the grocery store.

4. Broccoli

Broccoli is a member of the cabbage family. It has a unique taste and has many nutrients including calcium, potassium, carotenoids, phytonutrients, vitamin C, vitamin K, protein, iron, and potassium. This is why many people refer to it like a super vegetable. The carotenoids and fiber with the other nutrients keep diseases like cancer away. Fiber help with gut health and helps with weight loss.

Many people don't realize that broccoli is 90 percent water, three percent protein, and seven percent carbs. It doesn't contain any fat and is low in calories. One cup is only a total of 31 calories, so you get to eat it without worrying about gaining weight.

The carbs that are found in broccoli are mainly fiber and sugar. The sugar is mainly fructose and glucose with small amounts of lactose and maltose. Even with all that, the carb level is extremely low and only measures around 3.5 grams for each cup.

Plant compounds and trace elements that are found in broccoli include quercetin, carotenoids, sulforaphane, indole-3-carbinol, and antioxidants. These help with eye health, lower blood pressure, combat inflammation, and fight diseases.

5. Tomatoes

Tomatoes are a part of the nightshade family and are a native of South America. Many people think tomatoes are a vegetable, but the truth is they are a fruit. It is hard to believe that this wonderful fruit isn't a native of the Mediterranean since they are a staple in all Mediterranean dishes today. You won't find a dish that doesn't contain this wonderful fruit.

Tomatoes can be found in many forms like fresh, canned, and paste. They are rich in nutrients like vitamin C, bio-flavonoids, carotene, lycopene. Lycopene is a powerful antioxidant that fights against cancer most importantly prostate cancer. Tomatoes are very versatile and can be added to almost any recipe.

6. Wild Salmon

Many people don't realize that swapping a steak and ordering fish is an excellent idea. This is delicious and good for you. You need to make sure you choose wild salmon instead of farm-raised since farm raised is usually fed soy and don't have the benefits that wild salmon has. Research has shown that salmon is a very nutritious food. It can reduce the risk factors of many diseases.

It is full of omega 3 fatty acids. You will get about 2.5 grams in every 100 grams of 3.5 ounces. Omega 3 fatty acids are essential because our bodies can't create them. Many health experts suggest a daily intake of between 250 and 500 grams of omega 3 fatty acids that are rich in EPA and DHA. This is equal to eating two servings each week.

Farm raised salmon are full of omega 6 fatty acids that aren't good for you. If you want the best, go to your local fish market and ask for wild salmon. They have 39 grams of protein for each serving. Protein is essential to the body and needs to come from your diet.

7. Shrimp

Seafood is eaten in most of the communities that live along the Mediterranean coast. The most popular is shrimp. It is a good source of protein and very nutritious. Fish, shellfish, and seafood are all consumed due to their availability. These all contain omega 3 fatty acids.

Seafood like shrimp and squid give you the nutrients selenium, protein, and niacin. Shrimp is a type of shellfish, so if you have an allergy, please don't eat them. Shrimp includes other nutrients like phosphorus, zinc, magnesium, iron, phosphorus, vitamin B12, and iodine. It is a good source of iodine and antioxidants, too.

8. Garlic

Garlic is considered a superfood because it is packed with many nutrients. Hippocrates would prescribe garlic to treat different ailments. It is used to add flavor to many foods that are eaten in this lifestyle. Garlic can be put in many foods like vegetables and pasta.

This little plant works well with many foods. Garlic is full of manganese and vitamin B6. It is so powerful that it can get rid of fungus, bacteria, and viruses that are in the body. These health benefits have all been confirmed by science.

Garlic has many healing properties. It combats skin ailments, colds, and can regulate the heartbeat. It can lower bad cholesterol and improves good cholesterol. It is important to add garlic to meals.

9. Peppers

Cooking for the Mediterranean diet involves peppers. These can be used in many different ways including roasted, fresh, dried, and ground. They can be ground into various sauces and pastes to be used as flavorings to many different dishes.

In addition to flavor, they also give many different nutrients including beta-carotene, vitamin K, fiber, folate, vitamins A, and C. They contain zeaxanthin, lycopene, and lutein that give protection against macular degeneration.

10. Chickpeas

Beans are full of nutrients like iron, zinc, folate, and calcium. Chickpeas are a popular legume that can be eaten alone or with other foods. They also go by other names like Bengali gram and garbanzo beans. They are small, round, and cream colored and are popular in Africa, Asia, and the Mediterranean. They are combined with other grains, starches, and beans to make a healthy and delicious meal. They aren't only healthy, but they make you feel full.

Chickpeas contain soluble and insoluble fiber along with phytates and phytosterols. Chickpeas can help the body fight off diabetes, prevents colon cancer, and minimizes heart disease. Chickpeas are a staple food that is eaten regularly by ancient Greeks, Romans, and Egyptians.

Chickpeas are loved across the Mediterranean because they taste good and have many healthy fats, carbs, phosphorus, magnesium, phosphorus, zinc, iron, molybdenum, calcium, potassium, and vitamin Bs.

11. Chicken

Chicken is the most popular white meat there is. It is the most consumed meat. It is an excellent source of protein if you want to build lean muscles, maintain muscle mass, and lose fat.

You can grill, bake, and sear chicken. You shouldn't deep fry it. You can consume chicken until you are full. It is beneficial to your body since it contains lean protein that is needed to build muscle. You can create a whole meal based on vegetables and chicken or add in grains like rice or pasta.

12. Quinoa

The best way to enjoy quinoa is by fixing a delicious soup. Quinoa is gluten free and a great source of protein. One cup of this food has five grams of fiber and eight grams of protein. It contains many minerals and nutrients like calcium and magnesium, zinc, iron, copper, folate, phosphorus, manganese, fiber, and protein. It contains trace minerals such as quercetin, oxalates, and phytic acid.

It has a mild flavor and tastes pleasant when cooked in coconut milk or chicken stock. There is a bitter version that has more antioxidants when compared to the sweeter varieties. Both are an excellent source for antioxidants and minerals. Quinoa has the highest antioxidant content of most pulses, legumes, and cereals.

Quinoa gives you 16 percent protein dry weight. Quinoa contains fiber that is excellent for our digestive system. You get ten percent fiber per dry weight. Insoluble fiber can reduce the risk of diabetes while feeding the good bacteria in the gut.

13. Greek Yogurt

This strained yogurt is different from normal yogurt. When they make yogurt, they add in extra steps during the production. This process gets rid of excess lactose, minerals, and water. What is left is a creamy, rich yogurt that tastes tart, has lots of carbs and less sugar. Your body can absorb these nutrients easily due to the acidity.

Yogurt is popular with the residents along the Mediterranean Sea, especially Skyr and Greek yogurt. Skyr is an Icelandic yogurt. Greek yogurt uses goat milk while Skyr is sieved a lot and used more milk to increase the flavor and texture. Yogurts from that region only use natural ingredients like milk from cows, agave, and fruit. It doesn't contain any artificial flavors, sugars, and colors. You can sprinkle some chia seeds on your yogurt or add some to your soup.

The best way to eat this yogurt is plain with no added colorings or flavors. It has many health benefits and should be part of your normal diet. Yogurt contains potassium, calcium, probiotics, and proteins.

14. Chia Seeds

Chia seeds are loaded with many nutrients that provide vitamin C, calcium, manganese, fat, protein, magnesium, and fiber. 28 grams of chia seeds contains 30 percent manganese, 18 percent calcium, 9 grams of fat that contain omega 3, four grams of protein, and 11 grams of fiber. Chia seeds also have vitamin B2, zinc, potassium, vitamin B1, and vitamin B 3. One single ounce only has 137 calories with one gram of carbs.

They can keep you feeling fuller longer. You can add these to your diet many ways like adding them to a breakfast smoothie, oatmeal, and yogurt. They don't have much flavor, so they pair well with other foods.

15. Olive Oil

Extra virgin olive oil is the healthiest and best oil in the world. There has always been controversy about oils, especially seed oils and animal fats. People worry about the effect it will have on our bodies. When talking about olive oil, there isn't any controversy. Olive oil is popular when preparing vegetables.

Extra virgin olive oil is cold pressed directly from olives and is important for salad dressings and cooking. It is rich in antioxidants and monounsaturated fats. Scientists think olive oil is the main reason why people who live in the Mediterranean don't have heart disease. It can also help keep cancer at bay and reduce stubborn belly fat.

16. Eggplant

The eggplant is also called an aubergine and is another part of the nightshade family. It has a neutral flavor and texture. Many call it a vegetable but it is a fruit since it grows from a flowering plant and its seeds are inside. There are many varieties of eggplants, but the most common has deep purple skin.

It can be substituted for meat and is popular in many Mediterranean dishes. It does contain fiber and potassium along with phytonutrients and chlorogenic acid that gives it antiviral and cancer-fighting properties. It contains carbs, manganese, magnesium, folate, vitamin C, vitamin K, and protein. Trace elements include niacin and copper.

Eggplant is high in antioxidants that protect our bodies from illnesses such as heart disease and cancer. Eggplants are high in a pigment called anthocyanin. They protect against cell damage.

17. Hazelnuts

In Mediterranean countries, nut trees and olive trees are very common. This means that these products are readily available. Nuts are a healthy and delicious snack. Hazelnuts aren't just eaten as nuts but can be sprinkled on salads or ground up into sauces. They are usually eaten roasted or raw.

They are full of minerals, fats, and vitamins. They contain monounsaturated fats that are good for the heart. They contain protein, calcium, magnesium, fiber, and vitamin E. They are also rich in healthy fats, manganese, copper, thiamin, and carbs. They are a good source of poly and monounsaturated fats that contain the important omega 6 and 9 fatty acids.

18. Eggs

Eggs have been called nature's multivitamin since they are very nutritious. They can be eaten with most meals and have many benefits for your body. This is referring to the whole egg and not just the whites. Scientists have proven that the yolk is the best part of the egg. It contains choline that helps with losing weight. There are many ways to fix eggs including baking, boiled, omelets, scrambled, etc. Eggs are full of protein and good cholesterol.

Just one egg contains manganese, potassium, zinc, calcium, iron, vitamin E, folate, selenium, vitamins B2, B12, B5, vitamin A along with many trace minerals, and good fats.

19. Couscous

The base of many Mediterranean diets is unrefined grains like pasta, couscous, bread, and barley. When grains stay whole and unprocessed, their glycemic index stays low. They get digested slowly and go through the whole system slowly.

Couscous has been a delicacy for the people who are living in North Africa. It is an important part of the Mediterranean diet and is eaten around the world. There are three types of couscous. These are Israeli, Lebanese, and Moroccan. They all have the same benefits.

20. Ezekiel Bread

This is the healthiest bread you will find. This is a sprouted ancient grain bread that is baked from whole grains and legumes that have begun germinating. They contain no added sugars and are a better option than white bread and whole grain bread since these contain processed flours and added sugar. If you have to have bread, then choose Ezekiel bread. It is better for you. You can find various versions of this bread and some are flavored. One slice has three grams of fiber but only 80 calories.

Ezekiel bread contains different legumes and cereal grains. These grains include millet, spelt, wheat, and barley. The legumes are soybeans and lentils.

Foods to Avoid

When you are learning about a new lifestyle, you need to learn what foods that shouldn't be included. You need to learn to read food labels on everything. This is the only way to be aware of what is in the food you eat.

Here is a quick guide to help you out:

- Foods that are processed like bread and sausages need to be eaten in moderation.

- NEVER eat any that have been super processed like pastries, take out, and hot dogs. These are very high in sugar and salt. These ingredients have been proven to put you at risk for cancer.

- Check sugar content on anything that is labeled as low fat.

- DON'T add sugar to coffee or tea.

- ALWAYS check for sugar content isn't too high on the ingredients list. The higher it is on the list, the more it is in the food. Many readymade foods like bread, milk, and sauces contain it.

- STAY AWAY from foods that are made with refined grains. This means the processing has removed all the important fiber like white pasta, white rice, white flour, and white bread.

- STAY AWAY from refined oils and bad fats. Anything that is labeled as hydrogenated fats or trans fats are bad for you. These could be in foods like microwave popcorn, cakes, and margarine. Never use oils like soybean, soy, or canola. Find out what types of fats used in what you eat when you can.

- NEVER buy anything if it has trans fats on the label.

- Take out foods don't have labels on them but they contain a lot of trans fats. Be careful of them.

Eating Out

If you enjoy eating out, this doesn't mean you have to refrain from eating Mediterranean food. The Mediterranean lifestyle encourages making meals equal to a social event. You might need a night out with the girls to unwind. Their life might be slower, but there isn't any reason why you can't incorporate this into your new lifestyle. Here are some tips to help you when you are eating out:

- Stay away from salad dressings.

- When you sit down, drink a glass of water. Drinking water before a meal keeps you from overeating and will assist in weight loss.

- Choose a lot of vegetable and order more as a side dish.

- Stay away from breadbaskets. Eat whole wheat bread but save this for home.

- Stay away from sauces. They are full of salt and sugar to make them eatable.

- Stay away from anything that is deep fried unless you absolutely know they have been cooked in olive oil. You have to ask to find out.

- Choose chicken as the main entrée if you want a meat dish. Think about ordering fish or having a vegetarian plate.

- Don't order an appetizer or share one.

- Some portions at restaurants might be large. It is okay to leave food on your plate.

- Having fruit for dessert would be best. If you can't resist cake, cookies, or pies, share with friends.

- Sit down and enjoy yourself. Appreciate what you are eating and the people you are with.

- Have a glass of red wine and drink water for the rest of the meal.

- Be mindful when you eat. Don't just eat. Find the flavors inside.

- Chew slowly until everything in your mouth is masticated and easily swallowed.

Chapter 5: The 14-Day Diet Meal Plan

It is now time to start your Mediterranean diet. In this chapter, you will find a 14-day meal plan to help get you started. Every recipe in this meal plan can be found later on in the book, so you won't have to search for any recipes. You can start this any day of the week or at any time of the year. But you will likely find it easier to start this at the beginning of the week, either Sunday or Monday, and at a time of the year when you don't have any dining commitments. No matter when you decide to start this, you will be prepared and will love the results.

Week One

Day 1

Breakfast: Zucchini Frittata

Lunch: Humble Oatmeal

Dinner: Greek Meatballs

Day 2

Breakfast: Yogurt and Figs

Lunch: Cod and Shrimp Soup

Dinner: Mediterranean Potato and Zucchini Bake

Day 3

Breakfast: Nutty Oats and Apple

Lunch: Red Pepper Pasta

Dinner: Roasted Red Mullet Tomato Salad

Day 4

Breakfast: Lemon Scones

Lunch: Bean Salad

Dinner: Stuffed Pepper and Quinoa

Day 5

Breakfast: Fava Beans on Pita

Lunch: Stuffed Grape Leaves

Dinner: Ras-el-hanout Baked Chicken

Day 6

Breakfast: Sardine and Egg Artichoke

Lunch: Chicken and Couscous Burrito

Dinner: Eggplant Rolls with Salad

Day 7

Breakfast: Greek Yogurt with Fruit Salad

Lunch: Feta and Couscous Wrap

Dinner: Chicken Bake

Week Two

Day 8

Breakfast: Egg and Avocado on Toast

Lunch: Tuna Salad

Dinner: Roasted Lamb and Veggies

Day 9

Breakfast: Honey Yogurt and Melon

Lunch: Creamy Chicken Pita

Dinner: Chicken with Prunes and Rice

Day 10

Breakfast: Lemon Scone

Lunch: Whole Wheat Avocado and Cheese Sandwich

Dinner: Harissa Baked Cod and Bulgar

Day 11

Breakfast: Fruit Salad

Lunch: Chickpea and Pepper Salad

Dinner: Red Pepper Chicken and Quinoa

Day 12

Breakfast: Spinach and Tomato Frittata

Lunch: Buffet Bento

Dinner: Red Pepper Chicken and Quinoa

Day 13

Breakfast: Greek Yogurt and Berries

Lunch: Hummus and Chickpea Pita

Dinner: Salmon and Beet with Rice

Day 14

Breakfast: Scrambled Eggs and Spinach

Lunch: Tomato and Avocado Salad

Dinner: Cannelloni Bean Stew

Breakfast

Zucchini Frittata

Four servings

What You Will Need:

Pepper

Salt

EVOO, 1 tbsp

Milk, 2 tbsp

Minced garlic, 1 clove

Eggs, 8

Crumbled goat cheese, 2 oz

Sliced zucchini, 2

What You Do:

1. Add the oil to a skillet and sauté the zucchini and garlic for around five minutes.

2. Whisk together the milk and eggs and season with pepper and salt. Add the zucchini mixture to the eggs and stir everything together.

3. Pour the egg back into the pan and slide into a 350-degree oven. Allow it to bake for 10 to 15 minutes until the eggs are set.

4. Allow this to stand for three minutes. This will help it to come out of the pan easier.

5. Slice into quarters and enjoy.

Yogurt and Figs

Four servings

What You Will Need:

Cinnamon, 1 tsp

Honey, 2 tbsp

Greek yogurt, 2 c

Chopped pistachios, .25 c

Halved figs, 8 oz

What You Do:

1. Add a tablespoon of honey and the figs in a skillet. Place the figs cut side down and make sure that the honey covers the bottom of the pan. You want to make sure that the figs are in the honey. Allow them to cook for five minutes.

2. Split the yogurt between four bowls. Top the yogurt with the figs, a sprinkle of cinnamon, and the nuts. Drizzle the rest of the honey over the top.

Nutty Oats and Apple

One serving

What You Will Need:

Quick cooking oats, .25 c

Half of an apple, sliced and peeled

Skim milk, .5 c

Honey, 3 tbsp

Flaxseed, 1 tsp

Chopped walnuts, 2 tbsp

What You Do:

1. Place all of the ingredients into a microwave-safe bowl and mix together. Cook the mixture for a minute. Remove and stir the mixture together. Allow this to cook for another minute. Let it sit for a minute before serving.

Lemon Scones

12 servings

What You Will Need:

Salt, .5 tsp

Lemon juice, 2 tsp

Buttermilk, 3 oz

Baking soda, 2 tsp

Sugar, 2 tbsp

Butter, 3 oz

All-purpose flour, 7 oz

Frosting –

Lemon juice, 1-2 tsp

Powdered sugar, 1 c

What You Do:

1. Start by placing your oven to 400.

2. Mix together the salt, sugar, baking soda, and flour in a large bowl. Cut the butter into the mixture using a pastry cutter, two knives, or your clean hands. It should look like breadcrumbs.

3. Add in the buttermilk and lemon juice. Form the dough into a ball and then flatten the dough out on a floured surface to your desired thickness.

4. Slice the dough into 12 triangles. Place them on a baking sheet and allow them to cook for 12 minutes.

5. As they cook, mix together the lemon juice and powdered sugar until it comes together.

6. After the scones are cooked through, drizzle them with the frosting. Enjoy.

Fava Beans on Pita

Two servings

What You Will Need:

Pepper

Salt

EVOO, 1 tbsp

Water, .5 c

Juice of 2 lemons

Cumin, 1 tsp

Minced garlic, 2 cloves

Chopped onion, .5

Whole-wheat pita, 2

Rinse and drained fava beans, 16 oz

What You Do:

1. Add the oil to a pan and sauté the onions for around two minutes. Mix in the cumin and garlic and allow them to cook for another minute.

2. Stir in the water and the fava beans. Allow everything to come to a boil, turn the heat down, cover, and cook for ten minutes. Take the lid off and let it cook until most of the liquid has reduced.

3. Pour this into a bowl and add in the lemon juice. Crush up the mixture with a potato masher until it has reached your desired consistency.

4. Serve this on two warmed pita bread. You can also top this with a hardboiled egg.

Sardine and Egg Artichoke

Two servings

What You Will Need:

Pepper

Salt

Shredded lettuce, 1 c

Eggs, 2

Chopped artichoke hearts, 5 tbsp

Sardines in tomato sauce, 4 oz

What You Do:

1. Start by placing your oven to 400.

2. Place the artichokes and sardines in a small bowl and mash them into a lumpy paste.

3. Spread this mixture into a greased, small oven dish. Break the eggs on top, making sure you don't break the yolks.

4. Season with some pepper and salt and bake for ten minutes. Serve topped with lettuce.

Greek Yogurt with Fruit Salad

Two servings

What You Will Need:

Greek yogurt, 1 c

Fruit salad (one whole recipe found later in this chapter)

What You Do:

1. Fix the fruit salad according to the recipe below. Split the yogurt between two bowls and top with the fruit salad. Drizzle with some extra honey if desired.

Egg and Avocado on Toast

One serving

What You Will Need:

Pepper

Salt

Thinly sliced avocado, .5

Wholemeal bread, 1 slice

Egg, 1

What You Do:

1. Boil the egg until it reaches a medium soft consistency. This will take about eight minutes.

2. Toast your slice of bread and while it is still warm, top it with the avocado. Spread the avocado out with a knife.

3. After the egg has cooked, place it in cold water to stop the cooking and then peel the egg. Quarter it and place it on top of the avocado. Season with some pepper and salt.

Honey Yogurt and Melon

Eight servings

What You Will Need:

Honey, .25 c

Chopped mint, .5 c

Greek yogurt, 3 c

Honeydew melon sliced into 16 wedges

What You Do:

1. Divide the yogurt between eight bowls and drizzle it with honey and a garnish of mint. Serve with two slices of melon.

Fruit Salad

Two servings

What You Will Need:

Honey

Sliced toasted almonds, 14 oz

Sliced mint leaves, 8

Lemon juice, 1 tbsp

Halved grapes, 12 oz

Persimmons, 3

What You Do:

1. Peel the persimmons and cut them into wedges. Place all of the ingredients in a bowl and toss together. Drizzle on as much honey as you want.

Spinach and Tomato Frittata

Two servings

What You Will Need:

Pepper

Salt

EVOO, 1 tbsp

Dried oregano, 1 tsp

Crumbled feta, 1 tbsp

Chopped spinach, 1 c

Halved and pitted Greek olives, .5 c

Diced plum tomatoes, 3

Skim milk, 5 c

Eggs, 6

What You Do:

1. Start by placing your oven to 400.

2. Lightly beat the eggs and stir in the rest of the ingredients. Season it with some pepper and salt.

3. Grease an 8-inch pie pan and pour in the egg mixture. Bake the frittata for 20 minutes or until the eggs are completely set. Slice in half and enjoy.

Greek Yogurt and Berries

One serving

What You Will Need:

Greek yogurt, .5 c

Mixed berries, 1 c

Honey, 1 tbsp

Cinnamon

What You Do:

1. Place the yogurt in a bowl and top with the mixed berries, a drizzle of honey, and a sprinkle of cinnamon.

Scrambled Eggs and Spinach

One serving

What You Will Need:

Pepper

Salt

Chopped plum tomatoes, 2

Shredded spinach, 1 c

Butter, 1 tsp

Eggs, 2

What You Do:

1. Place the butter in a pan and allow to melt. Add in the tomatoes and spinach. Cook until the spinach has wilted.

2. Beat the eggs together and pour into the pan over the tomatoes and spinach. Scramble everything together. Season the mixture with pepper and salt to taste. Enjoy.

Breakfast Wrap

Two servings

What You Will Need:

Basil, 1.5 tsp

Egg substitute, 1 c

Baby spinach, .5 c

Tomato

Onion, .25 c

Red pepper, .25 c

Olive oil, 1 tbsp

Feta, 2 tbsp

Wheat tortillas, 2

What You Do:

1. Start by heating the oil in a skillet and then add in the onion and pepper.

2. Cook over medium until they are both soft.

3. Next, add in the spices and egg substitute. Cook until the eggs are cooked all the way through.

4. Once the eggs have cooked through, place the egg, tomato, and spinach on the wrap. Add on the feta and wrap up.

Mediterranean Scramble

One serving

What You Will Need:

Pepper

Salt

Cubed feta, 2 tbsp

Eggs, 3

Baby spinach, 1 c

Diced and seeded tomato, .33 c

Vegetable oil, 1 tbsp

What You Do:

1. Add the oil to a frying pan and heat.

2. Add in the spinach and tomatoes, cooking until the spinach has wilted.

3. Add in the eggs and scramble them. After about 30 seconds, mix in the feta. Continue to cook until the eggs are fully cooked.

4. Season with some pepper and salt.

Mediterranean Egg Salad

Four servings

What You Will Need:

Pepper

Salt, .5 tsp

Cumin, .25 tsp

Oregano, 1.5 tsp

Lemon juice

Greek yogurt, .5 c

Chopped olives, .25 c

Chopped cucumber, .5 c

Chopped red onion, .5 c

Chopped sun-dried tomato, .5 c

Hardboiled eggs, 8

What You Do:

1. Chop up the hardboiled eggs and place them in a bowl.

2. Add in the olives, cucumber, red onion, and tomatoes, tossing everything together.

3. Stir the spices, splash of lemon juice, and Greek yogurt together. Pour over the egg mixture and stir to coat.

4. This will keep for a week refrigerated.

Lunch

Humble Oatmeal

One serving

What You Will Need:

Pepper

Salt

EVOO, 1 tbsp

Vegetable broth, 1 c

Dried oregano, .5 tsp

Minced garlic, 1 clove

Crumbled feta, .25 c

Chopped sun-dried tomatoes, .25 c

Pitted and halved olives, .25 c

Oatmeal, .5 c

What You Do:

1. Add the broth to a large pan and allow it to come to a boil.

2. Add in the pepper, salt, oregano, and oatmeal. Let this simmer for five minutes, stirring occasionally.

3. Add a half of a tablespoon of oil to a skillet and cook the olives, tomatoes, and garlic for three minutes.

4. Add the oatmeal mixture to a bowl and top it with the olive mixture. Sprinkle it with some feta and drizzle of a tablespoon of oil.

Cod and Shrimp Soup

Four servings

What You Will Need:

Pepper

Salt

EVOO, 1 tbsp

Dry white wine, .25 c

Chopped parsley, .25 c

Chicken broth, 1 c

Dried oregano, 1 tsp

Minced garlic, 1 clove

Sliced celery, 2 stalks

Chopped onion

Tomato puree, 10 oz

Diced tomatoes, 14 oz

Deveined and sliced lengthwise shrimp, 6 oz

Cod fillet cubes, 8 oz

What You Do:

1. In a large skillet, add in the oil and cook the celery and onion together for two minutes. Stir in the garlic and cook for another minute.

2. Add in the wine and broth. Allow everything to come to a boil and then simmer for five minutes. Add in the pepper, salt, oregano, tomato puree, and tomatoes. Allow it to come back to a boil. Turn the heat down and let it simmer. Place on the lid and cook for five minutes.

3. Bring it back up to a boil and add in the fish and shrimp. Turn the heat back down and let it simmer for another five minutes.

4. After the fish is cooked through, flake it apart with a fork and serve with a sprinkling of parsley.

Red Pepper Pasta

Six servings

What You Will Need:

Pepper

Salt

EVOO, 2 tbsp

Dried basil, .5 tsp

Minced garlic, 1 clove

Red wine vinegar, 1 tbsp

Mayonnaise, .25 c

Greek yogurt, .25 c

Chopped white onion, 2 oz

Grated carrot, 8 oz

Diced red bell pepper, 8 oz

Chopped tomatoes, 8 oz

Chopped and pitted olives, 2 oz

Whole-wheat pasta, 16 oz

What You Do:

1. Cook your pasta according to the directions on the package.

2. Whisk together the mayonnaise and yogurt. Add in the garlic, vinegar, oil, pepper, and salt.

3. Drain the pasta once cooked and then pour the yogurt mixture over it and toss together. Add in all of your vegetables and toss together.

4. This can be served cold or warm.

Bean Salad

Two servings

What You Will Need:

Pepper

Salt

EVOO, .25 c

Red wine vinegar, 2 tbsp

Dijon mustard, 1 tsp

Chopped parsley, .5 c

Chopped red onion, 3 tbsp

Cooked cannelloni beans, 1.5 c

What You Do:

1. Place the onions in cold water and allow them to soak for ten minutes.

2. Whisk together the oil, vinegar, and mustard in a small bowl. Drain the onions and add them to the mustard mixture. Stir in the pepper, salt, parsley, and beans.

3. Allow this to marinate in the refrigerator for 20 minutes to allow the dressing to soak into the beans and other veggies.

Stuffed Grape Leaves

Five servings

What You Will Need:

Pepper

Salt

EVOO, 2 tbsp

Chopped parsley, .5 c

Tahini, 3 tbsp

Lemon juice, .5 c

Zest of 1 lemon

Minced garlic, 7 cloves

Chopped white onion

Cooked bulgur wheat, 1 c

Drained and washed chickpeas, 19 oz

Drained grape leaves, 15 oz jar

What You Do:

1. Boil some water in a pot and turn the temp down to medium so that it simmers. Unroll the grape leaves and carefully add the whole leaves into the water so that they can cook. You can use any of the broken leaves for later use. Take the leaves out of the water after they have boiled for five minutes.

2. Add the chickpeas to a food processor and chop them up to a rough consistency. Set them to the side.

3. In the cleaned-out food processor, mix together the pepper, salt, tahini, garlic, and the lemon juice and zest. Mix until they form a smooth paste. Add in the onions, parsley, bulgur, and chickpeas.

4. Flatten out the grape leaves and add about one to two teaspoons of the chickpea mixture. Fold the ends of the leaves in and then roll them up so that they form a rectangular type shape.

5. Place part of the broken grape leaves in the bottom of a large pot. Make sure that the pot is covered. Tuck as many of the stuffed grape leaves into the pot as you can fit. Drizzle in two tablespoons of lemon juice. Repeat with a second layer, adding the broken leaves and then place the stuffed leaves on top, again, drizzling with lemon juice. Put a heatproof plate over the stuffed grape leaves.

6. Lay a heatproof bowl filled ¾ full with water on top of the plate. This will work as a weight.

7. Pour water into the pot until it comes up to the plate. The stuffed grape leaves need to be completely submerged. Allow the water to come to a boil. Allow them to simmer for 30 minutes.

8. Serve the stuffed grape leaves with a lemon wedge and some tzatziki sauce for dipping.

9. These can be frozen or they will need to be kept in an airtight container for three days. To reheat, add to hot water.

Chicken and Couscous Burrito

Four servings

What You Will Need:

10-inch tomato or spinach tortilla, 4

Pepper

Salt

EVOO, 2 tbsp

Lemon juice, .25 c

Chopped parsley, 1 c

Chopped mint, .25 c

Minced garlic, 1 tsp

Chopped and peeled cucumber, 1 c

Chopped medium tomato

Cubed chicken breast, 1 lb

Whole-wheat couscous, .33 c

What You Do:

1. Add the couscous to a small pot and cover with boiling water. Place on a lid and set it to the side for five minutes.

2. In a bowl, add in the pepper, salt, garlic, oil, lemon juice, mint, and parsley. Whisk everything together until well combined. Add the chicken pieces in a bowl and add in a tablespoon of the mint mixture and toss to coat.

3. Heat a skillet and add in the chicken. Cook about three to five minutes on both sides.

4. Fluff the couscous with a fork and pour in the rest of the mix mixture, cucumber, and tomato

5. Place ¾ cup of couscous on each of the wraps. Divide the chicken between each of the wraps. Roll up and tuck the ends in. Slice in half and enjoy.

Feta and Couscous Wrap

Four servings

What You Will Need:

Pepper

Salt

EVOO, 2 tbsp

Lemon juice, 2 tbsp

Boiling water, .5 c

Sun-dried tomato wraps, 4

Diced cucumber

Diced tomato

Sliced red bell peppers, 2

Minced garlic, 2 cloves

Crumbled feta, 1 c

Whole-wheat couscous, .5 c

What You Do:

1. Bring some water to a boil. Once boiling, remove from heat and add in the couscous, stir, and cover with a lid. Allow this to sit for five minutes.

2. To make the dressing, mix together the olive oil, lemon juice, pepper, salt, mint, and garlic. Whisking until everything has come together.

3. Once the couscous is cooked, mix together the couscous, feta, tomato, and cucumber and stir into the dressing.

4. Divide the mixture between the four wraps and roll them up, making sure the ends are folded in.

5. Serve alongside a simple salad sprinkled with a bit of olive oil.

Tuna Salad

Two servings

What You Will Need:

Pepper

Salt

EVOO

Lemon juice, 2 tbsp

Chopped scallion – only the green part

Minced celery, .5 stalk

Chopped basil, 1 tbsp

Drained tuna packed in oil, 5 oz

What You Do:

1. Add the tuna to a small bowl and break it up into small pieces using a fork.

2. Add in the lemon juice, scallions, celery, and basil. With a fork, stir all of the ingredients together until they are well mixed.

3. Moisten the tuna to your liking with some olive oil. Usually, one to two tablespoons will work. Season with some pepper and salt to your taste.

Creamy Chicken Pita

Two servings

What You Will Need:

EVOO, 1 tbsp

Dried oregano, .5 tsp

Cubed cucumber, .5

Garlic clove

Diced medium tomato

Chunked chicken breast

Whole-wheat pita, 2

Marinade –

Pepper

Salt

EVOO, 1 tbsp

Dried oregano, 1 tsp

Greek yogurt, .5 c

Greek Sauce –

Sugar, .25 tsp

Lemon juice, .5 tsp

White wine vinegar, 1 tbsp

Milk, 1 tbsp

Mayonnaise, 2 tbsp

Pepper

Salt

Pinch garlic powder

What You Do:

1. Whisk the pepper, salt, a teaspoon of oregano, a tablespoon of oil, and yogurt together in a medium bowl. Add in the chicken and toss together so that it is thoroughly coated. Marinate the chicken for at least two hours. It is best if you can let it marinate overnight.

2. To make the Greek sauce, whisk everything together and then keep it stored in the fridge.

3. Take the chicken out of the marinade.

4. Add a tablespoon of oil to a skillet. Add in the chicken and let it cook until almost cooked through.

5. Stir in the oregano and garlic. Cook for another six minutes or until the chicken is cooked through.

6. Once cooked, add the chicken to the Greek sauce and toss. Divide chicken mixture between the pita bread and top with the cucumber and tomatoes.

Whole Wheat Avocado and Cheese Sandwich

One serving

What You Will Need:

Quartered pear

Balsamic vinegar, 2 tsp

Shredded lettuce and spinach, 1 c

Sliced medium tomato

Mashed avocado, .25 c

Grated parmesan, .25 c

Whole-wheat bread, 2 slices

What You Do:

1. Spread the avocado across one of the slices of bread. Sprinkle it with some cheese and then top it with some tomatoes.

2. Place both slices of bread under the broiler. Allow them to cook until the bare slice has browned and the cheese on the other slice has melted.

3. Add on the greens and drizzle on the balsamic vinegar. Top the sandwich with the bare slice of bread and press together.

4. Slice in half and serve alongside the pear.

Chickpea and Pepper Salad

Four servings

What You Will Need:

Crumbled feta, 1 c

Pitted and halved olives, .5 c

Diced small red onion

Diced red bell pepper

Diced cucumber

Halved cherry tomatoes, 2 c

Drained and washed chickpeas, 1.5 c

Dressing –

Pepper

Salt

Chopped parsley, .5 c

Dried oregano, .25 tsp

Lemon juice, .25 c

EVOO, 2 tbsp

What You Do:

1. To make the dressing, add all of the ingredients to a jar with a lid and shake well until everything has mixed together.

2. To make the salad, place all of the ingredients in a bowl and mix everything together.

3. Drizzle the dressing over the salad and toss everything together.

4. It is best if you allow everything to marinade for about ten minutes before you serve it.

Buffet Bento

One serving

What You Will Need:

Pepper

Red wine vinegar, 1 tsp

EVOO, .5 tsp

Chopped parsley, 1 tbsp

Quartered whole-wheat pita

Crumbled feta, 1 oz

Hummus, 2 tbsp

Pitted and halved olives, 1 c

Grapes, 1 c

Halved cherry tomatoes, .25 c

Diced cucumber, .25 c

Cubed and cooked chicken breast, 3 oz

Drained and rinsed chickpeas, .25 c

What You Do:

1. Mix together the pepper, vinegar, olives, parsley, feta, tomatoes, and cucumber. Cover with a lid.

2. Place the pita, grapes, chicken, and the hummus in their own containers and cover them.

3. These can be packed up in a lunch box, and once you are ready to eat, open the containers and enjoy.

Hummus and Chickpea Pita

One serving

What You Will Need:

Pepper

Salt

EVOO, 1 tbsp

Pitted and chopped olives, 2 tsp

Drained and rinsed baby spinach, a handful

Shredded carrots, .25 c

Sun-dried tomatoes, 2 tsp

Crumbled feta, 2 tbsp

Drained and rinsed chickpeas, .25 c

Hummus, .25 c

Whole-wheat pita, cut in half

What You Do:

1. Warm the pita and open up the pocket. Divide the hummus, olives, spinach, tomatoes, carrots, and chickpeas into each pocket. Drizzle them with some oil and top with the feta, pepper, and salt.

2. You can refrigerate these for up to four hours.

Tomato and Avocado Salad

Four servings

What You Will Need:

Chopped parsley, 2 sprigs

Halved and pitted olives, 3.5 oz

Crumbled feta, 4 oz

Diced small red onion

Quartered cherry tomatoes, 10 oz

Sliced and peeled cucumber

Chopped avocado

Dressing –

Pepper

Salt

Sugar, .25 tsp

Dried oregano, .25 tsp

Minced garlic clove

Red wine vinegar, 2 tbsp

EVOO, 2 tbsp

What You Do:

1. To make the dressing, add all of the ingredients into a jar with a lid. Shake the contents until they are well combined.

2. To make the salad, toss the parsley, onion, cucumber, olives, tomatoes, and avocado together in a bowl.

3. Drizzle the dressing over the salad and toss together.

4. Top with the cheese. It is best if you let everything marinate for ten minutes before serving.

Falafel Bowls

Four servings

What You Will Need:

Crumbled feta, .25 c

Pitted Kalamata olives, .25 c

Tahini sauce, .5 c

Steam-in-bag fresh green beans, 16 oz

Whole-wheat couscous, .5 c

Water, .66 c

Frozen prepared falafel, 8 oz pack

What You Do:

1. Follow the directions on the package of falafels to cook them. Set them to the side to cool.

2. Bring a small pot of water up to a boil. Mix in the couscous, place on the lid, and set it off the heat. Allow this to stand until the liquid has absorbed, around five minutes. Fluff with a fork and then set to the side.

3. Follow the directions on the package of green beans to cook them.

4. Divide your tahini sauce between four small condiment containers with lids and place them in the refrigerator.

5. Split the green beans between four single-serving containers that have lids. Top each of these with a half of a cup of couscous, a fourth of a falafel, along with a tablespoon of feta and a tablespoon of olives. Place a lid on the containers and refrigerate them. They can be kept for up to four days.

6. To serve, reheat everything in the microwave for about two minutes. Dress everything with the tahini sauce.

Lettuce Wraps

Four servings

What You Will Need:

Sliced shallots, .5 c

Drained roasted red peppers, .5 c

Rinsed chickpeas, 2 15-oz cans

Paprika, .5 tsp

Salt, .75 tsp

Maple syrup, 1.5 tsp

Lemon juice, .25 c

Lemon zest, 1 tsp

EVOO, .25 c

Tahini, .25 c

Chopped parsley, 2 tbsp

Chopped toasted almonds, .25 c

Bibb lettuce leaves, 12 large

What You Do:

1. Whisk together the paprika, salt, maple syrup, lemon juice, lemon zest, oil, and tahini in a large bowl. Once combined, stir in the shallots, peppers, and chickpeas. Make sure everything is coated.

2. Split the mixture between the lettuce leaves, around a third of a cup in each one. Top with the parsley and almonds. Wrap the leaves around the filling and enjoy.

Dinner

Greek Meatballs

Five servings

What You Will Need:

Pepper

Salt

EVOO, 2 tbsp

Red pepper flakes, .5 tsp

Cinnamon, .5 tsp

Cumin, 1 tbsp

Ground cloves, .5 tsp

Ground coriander, 1 tbsp

Dried mint, .5 tsp

Dried parsley, 1 tsp

Grated garlic, 2 cloves

Dried ginger, 1 tbsp

Chopped red onion, .5

Whole wheat pita, 5

Ground beef, 1 lb

Tzatziki –

Pepper

Salt

EVOO, 2 tbsp

Dried mint, 1 tsp

Chopped dill, .5 c

Grated garlic, 1 clove

Greek yogurt, 1 c

Juice and zest of lemon, 2

Grated onion, .5

Cucumber

What You Do:

1. You want to make the tzatziki sauce first so that the flavors can marinate.

2. Dice a quarter of the cucumber. Peel and grate the rest of the cucumber. Put the grated cucumber in a bowl and sprinkle with some salt. Allow this to set for 15 minutes.

3. In a separate bowl, mix together the oil, mint, dill, garlic, two tablespoons of lemon juice, and a tablespoon of lemon zest. Season with some pepper and salt.

4. Back to the grated cucumber. Place that cucumber in some cheesecloth and squeeze out the excess liquid. Mix this into the yogurt mixture. Let this chill in the fridge for at least an hour.

5. For the meatballs – Mix together the cinnamon, cumin, cloves, coriander, ground beef, mint, parsley, garlic, ginger, and onion. Season with some pepper and salt. Make sure that you mix well, but don't overwork it. Divide the mixture into 30 balls.

6. Heat oil in a pan and fry up the meatballs a few at a time until they are all browned and cooked through. As you cook some up, place them on a baking tray in a warm oven to keep them warm.

7. Warm the pitas up, making sure that you don't brown them too much. Place the meatball on the pitas and garnish it with the tzatziki sauce, the diced cucumber, and the red onion.

Mediterranean Potato and Zucchini Bake

Four servings

What You Will Need:

Pepper

Salt

EVOO, 4 tbsp

Water, .5 c

Tomato paste, 4 tbsp

Sliced small onions,

Sliced large zucchinis, 8

Sliced peeled potatoes, 2 lb

What You Do:

1. Start by placing your oven to 400.

2. Grease a 9x12 baking dish.

3. Lay the zucchini, onions, and potatoes into the bottom of the dish and toss together.

4. Add in the tomato puree and water to a bowl and stir until everything is well blended. Pour this over the potato mixture.

5. Stir in some pepper, salt, and the olive oil. Allow this to bake for an hour and a half. Check on the dish every 30 minutes.

6. If it starts to look dry, add some more water. Once cooked through, enjoy as is or serve it as a side dish.

Roasted Red Mullet Tomato Salad

One serving

What You Will Need:

Minced garlic, 1 clove

Chopped thyme, 1 tbsp

Juice of half of a lemon

Juice of half of an orange

Red mullets, 2

Salad –

Sea salt, 1 tsp

Chopped mint leaves, 5

Pitted olives, 2 oz

Broad beans, 4 oz

Lemon juice, 1 tsp

Sliced fennel, 2 oz

Plum tomatoes, 6 oz

Dressing –

Lemon juice

EVOO, 1 tbsp

Chopped oregano, 1 tsp

What You Do:

1. Start by placing your oven to 425.

2. Cut two lines into the side of the fish.

3. Whisk together the garlic, chopped thyme, orange juice, and lemon juice. Pour this mixture over the mullets. Make sure you turn the fish to make

sure that it is completely covered. Lay in an ovenproof dish. Allow this to bake for 12 minutes or until it has cooked all the way through.

4. Mix all of the salad ingredients together and sprinkle it with some salt. Place in the fridge for five minutes.

5. Mix all of the dressing ingredients together in a jar, shaking until emulsified. Pour the dressing over the salad and toss everything together until coated.

6. Once the fish is cooked, serve alongside the salad.

Stuffed Pepper and Quinoa

Four servings

What You Will Need:

Pepper

Salt

EVOO, 2 tbsp

Chopped parsley, 2 tbsp

Cooked quinoa, 16 oz

Crumbled feta, 3 oz

Chopped olives, .25 c

Sliced zucchini

Chopped white onion, .5 c

Halved and deseeded red bell peppers, 4

What You Do:

1. Start by placing your oven to 350.

2. Lay the halved peppers with the cut side up on a baking sheet. Season with some pepper and salt and then drizzle with a tablespoon of oil. Bake these for about 15 minutes.

3. Add a tablespoon of oil to a pan and heat. Add the zucchini and onions. Once the onions have become soft, take the pan off the heat and stir in the cooked quinoa, pepper, salt, parsley, feta, and olives.

4. Divide this mixture between the pepper halves. Place back in the oven and let them cook for another five minutes.

5. Serve with a salad.

Ras-el-hanout Baked Chicken

Four servings

What You Will Need:

Pepper

Salt

EVOO, 1 tbsp

Dried thyme, 1 tsp

Dried cilantro, 1 tsp

Ras-el-hanout, 2 tsp

Greek yogurt, 4 tbsp

Quartered lemon

Whole garlic, 3 cloves

Large red onion cut into wedges

Cubed carrots, 1 lb

Cubed and peeled sweet potatoes, 1 lb

Boned and skinned chicken breasts, 4

What You Do:

1. Start by placing your oven to 400.

2. Lay the sweet potatoes and carrots on a baking sheet and drizzle with some olive oil. Allow this to bake for ten minutes. Take it out of the oven and add on the garlic and red onion. Let this bake for another 20 minutes.

3. Slide the veggies to one side of the tray and lay the lemon quarters and chicken breasts on the other side. Bake until the chicken has reached 165 degrees, about 15 to 20 minutes.

4. Split the chicken and veggies between four plates and serve with a tablespoon of yogurt on top.

Eggplant Rolls with Salad

Two to three servings

What You Will Need:

Pepper

Salt

EVOO, 1 tbsp

Chopped basil, .25 c

Minced garlic, 2 cloves

Pitted green olives, 8

Tomato paste, 7 oz

Chopped tomatoes, 6

Thickly sliced zucchini

Thinly sliced red bell pepper

Cubed mozzarella, 1 c

Sliced white onion

Large eggplant

What You Do:

1. Start by placing your oven to 350.

2. Remove the skin from the eggplant and finely dice the skins.

3. Slice the eggplant, lengthwise, into long strips that are about an eighth of an inch thick.

4. Brush the slice with olive oil and fry them on a skillet for two to three minutes on both sides, or until it becomes tender. Remove from the pan and set to the side.

5. In the same pan, add in the rest of the oil and fry up the sliced zucchini, red peppers, half of the garlic, onions, and the diced eggplant skin. Cook

until everything is softened. Add in the paste, along with the pepper and salt and allow everything to come to a boil. Let this cook for ten minutes.

6. In a bowl, mix together the remaining garlic, mozzarella, basil, olives, and tomatoes. Spread out the eggplant slices and evenly divided the cooked mixture at the end of each one. Roll the eggplant up.

7. Place them in a casserole dish and top with the mozzarella and tomato mixture. Bake these until the cheese has melted. Make sure to serve them hot.

Chicken Bake

Four servings

What You Will Need:

Pepper

Salt

EVOO, 2 tsp

Dried tarragon, 1 tbsp

Garlic and herbs, soft cheese, 3 oz

Pitted black olives, 4

Cherry tomatoes, 6 oz

Quartered red onion

Chunked red bell peppers, 2

Skin-on chicken breasts, 4

What You Do:

1. Place your oven on 400.

2. Heat a teaspoon of oil in a skillet and add in the onions and peppers. Sauté the veggies for two minutes. Lay these onto a lined baking tray and place in the oven to cook for ten minutes.

3. Lift up the skin on the chicken breasts and push the soft cheese underneath it. Brush the skin tops with the remaining oil. Sprinkle the tarragon over the chicken.

4. Take the peppers and onions from the oven. Add on the olives and tomatoes and scoot the veggies to the side. Lay the chicken on the other side.

5. Place back in the oven and allow them to cook for 25 minutes. Once the chicken reaches 165 degrees, serve the chicken and veggies drizzled with some of the pan drippings.

Roasted Lamb and Veggies

Four servings

What You Will Need:

Pepper

Salt

EVOO, 2 tbsp

Dried mint, 1 tbsp

Dried thyme, 1 tbsp

Sliced zucchinis, 2

Chopped bell peppers, 2

Cubed sweet potato

Quartered red onion

Lamb cutlets, 8

What You Do:

1. Start by placing your oven to 400.

2. Add the oil to a pan and heat before adding in the sweet potatoes. Sauté for two minutes and then add in the zucchini, pepper, and red onions, sauté for two more minutes.

3. Lay this onto a prepared baking sheet. Season with some pepper and salt. Allow this to bake for five minutes. Take it out of the oven and slide the vegetables to one side of the tray.

4. Trim any of the excess fat you see on the lamb. Rub the lamb with a mixture of pepper, salt, mint, and thyme. Lay the lam on the empty side of the tray and place it back in the oven to bake for ten more minutes.

5. Remove and flip the lamb over. Allow this all to cook for ten minutes.

6. When serving, drizzle with some of the pan drippings.

Chicken with Prunes and Rice

Four servings

What You Will Need:

Long grain rice, 1 c

Pepper

Salt

Brown sugar, 1 tbsp

Red wine vinegar, 3 tbsp

White wine, .33 c

Dried oregano, 1 tsp

Minced garlic, 3 cloves

Chopped parsley, .25 c

Pitted green olives, 1.33 c

Chopped white onion

Cubed small carrot

Capers, 1 tbsp

Pitted prunes, .5 c

Chicken thighs, 4

Chicken legs, 4

What You Do:

1. In a crock pot, add the pepper, salt, oregano, sugar, vinegar, and white wine and stir together. Mix in the olives, prunes, capers, and garlic.

2. Place the chicken pieces on top of the mixture. Place the lid on the cooker and turn to low and cook for five to six hours or place it on high for three to four hours.

3. When there is a half hour left, mix in the parsley. At this time, start to cook the rice according to the instructions on the packet.

4. Serve the chicken mixture over the rice and top with some extra sauce.

Harissa Baked Cod and Bulgar

Two to three servings

What You Will Need:

Pepper

Salt

EVOO, 1 tsp

Dried cilantro, 1 tsp

Harissa paste, 2 tsp

Greek yogurt, 2 tbsp

Bulgur wheat, 2 oz

Lemon

Sliced green onions, 3

Chopped yellow pepper

Quarter tomatoes, 2

Cauliflower florets, 1 head

Cod fillet, 2 large

What You Do:

1. Start by setting your oven to 400.

2. Add a tablespoon of oil to a skillet and heat. Add the cauliflower and yellow pepper. Let this sauté for two minutes.

3. Prepare a baking sheet, and add the sauté vegetables and the tomatoes on the baking sheet and mix together. Allow this to roast for 15 minutes.

4. Add a cup of water to a small pan and allow it to come to a boil. Remove this from the heat and add in the bulgur wheat. Allow this to simmer for two minutes. Remove it from the heat and allow it to stand.

5. Slice the lemon in half. Squeeze the juice from one of the halves and then thinly slice the other half.

6. Take the veggies out of the oven once they are cooked. Add the green onions and bulgur wheat to the baking sheet and season with pepper, salt, and cilantro. Mix everything together and drizzle with some of the lemon juice. Make sure that you reserve some of the juice.

7. Coat your fish with the Harissa paste and lay the fish on top of the bulgur mixture. Allow the fish to bake until the fish is cooked all the way through. The fish should flake easily with a fork.

8. Add the remaining lemon juice over the fish.

9. Serve with some Greek yogurt.

Red Pepper Chicken and Quinoa

Four servings

What You Will Need:

Pepper

Salt

EVOO, 2 tbsp

Chopped parsley, 2 tbsp

Ground cumin, .5 tsp

Paprika, 1 tsp

Minced garlic, 1 tsp

Sliced almonds, .25 c

Crumbled feta, .25 c

Chopped olives, .25 c

Diced cucumber, 1 c

Chopped red onion, .5 c

Jarred roasted peppers, 7 oz

Cooked quinoa, 2 c

Boneless, skinless cubed chicken breast, 1 lb

What You Do:

1. Start by placing the oven to 425.

2. Line a baking tray with parchment paper and lay out the chicken. Sprinkle the chicken with pepper and salt.

3. Place the chicken in the oven for eight minutes and then rotate the tray and bake for an additional eight minutes.

4. Place a tablespoon of oil, cumin, paprika, garlic, almonds, and roasted peppers to a food processor and mix until smooth.

5. Stir together the remaining oil, olives, onions, and cooked quinoa in a bowl.

6. Divide the quinoa between three bowls and top with the cucumber. Top with the chicken and the roasted pepper puree.

7. Garnish the dish with some feta and parsley.

Salmon and Beet with Rice

Four servings

What You Will Need:

Pepper

Salt

EVOO, 2 tbsp

Chopped parsley, .25 c

Chopped pistachios, 1 tbsp

Dried basil, .5 tsp

Dried rosemary, .5 tsp

Minced garlic, 2 tsp

Lemon

Diced white onion

Cubed small carrot

Wild rice, 1 c

Halved Brussels sprouts, 8 oz

Medium golden beets, 2 – chopped into ½ -inch chunks

Salmon fillet slices, 4

What You Do:

1. Start by place your oven to 425.

2. Following the instructions on the rice to cook.

3. To a bowl, add a tablespoon of oil along with the beets, Brussels sprouts, pepper, and salt. Toss everything together and lay on a baking sheet. Roast in the oven for ten minutes.

4. Cut half of the lemon into thin slices.

5. Slide the veggies to one side. Add the salmon fillets to the other side of the baking tray with the vegetables and sprinkle the salmon with rosemary, pepper, and salt. Lay the slices of lemon over the salmon.

6. Roast this for another ten minutes or less, depending on how long it takes for the salmon to get cooked through.

7. Squeeze the juice of the remaining half of a lemon into a bowl. Add the garlic, pepper, salt, basil, and the remaining oil. Whisk everything together.

8. Once the veggies and salmon are cooked through, place the rice on a plate and top with the vegetables and then the salmon. Drizzle everything with the lemon juice mixture and sprinkle on some pistachios.

Cannellini Bean Stew

Six servings

What You Will Need:

Paprika, 1 tsp

Dried oregano, 1 tsp

Whole-wheat farro, 1 c

Minced garlic, 3 cloves

Tomato paste, 2 tbsp

Roughly chopped red bell pepper

Chopped tomatoes, 15 oz

Drained and rinsed cannellini beans, 15 oz

Chopped kale, 4 c

Chopped onion

Sliced celery, 2 stalks

Diced carrots, 2

Crumbled feta, 4 oz

Pepper

Salt

Vegetable broth, 5 c

Lemon juice, 1 tbsp

Fresh parsley, .5 c

Bay leaves, 2

What You Do:

1. Add oil to a large pot and heat.

2. Add in the onion, celery, and carrots. Cook them for about three minutes. Add in the tomato paste and garlic. Add in the tomatoes and broth.

3. Mix in the pepper, salt, bay leaves, paprika, oregano, farro, and bell peppers. Allow the mixture to come to a boil and lay the parsley on top. Once it has come to a boil, lower the heat, and allow to simmer for 15 minutes.

4. Take the pot off of the heat and discard the sprigs of parsley. Mix in the kale.

5. Place back on the heat and allow it to simmer for another 15 minutes.

6. Once the farro is cooked through, remove the pot from the heat and add in the cannelloni beans. Allow the stew to stand as the beans warm through and the farro continues to swell.

7. Add in some hot water if the consistency becomes too thick for you.

8. Take out the bay leaves and stir in the lemon juice before you serve it. Sprinkle with some feta for serving.

Lemon-Garlic Shrimp

12 servings

What You Will Need:

Salt, 5 tsp

Olive oil, 2 tbsp

Parsley, .25 c

Lemon juice, .25 c

Minced garlic, 3 tbsp

Shrimp, 1.25 lb

Pepper, .5 tsp

What You Do:

1. Start by heating a small pan over medium. Place the oil and garlic into the pan and cook for a minute.

2. Next, add in the pepper, salt, lemon juice, and parsley.

3. Last, add in the shrimp to a large bowl and pour the heated mixture over the shrimp.

4. Chill the shrimp until you are ready to serve.

Roasted Mediterranean Chicken

Four servings

What You Will Need:

Olive oil, 1 tbsp

Minced garlic, 2 cloves

Chopped bell pepper, .5 c

Sliced red onion

Sliced mushrooms, 8 oz

Boneless skinless chicken thighs or breasts, 1.5 lbs

Pepper, .25 tsp

Salt, .25 tsp

Chopped rosemary, 1 tsp

Chopped basil, 1 tbsp

Chopped oregano, 1 tbsp

Chopped parsley, 2 tbsp

Balsamic vinegar, 2 tbsp

Kalamata olives, 10

Cherry tomatoes, 1 c

Drained and rinsed cannellini beans, 15 oz

Asparagus spears cut into three-inch pieces, 1 lb

What You Do:

1. Start by placing your oven to 425. Line two baking sheets with foil and set to the side.

2. Mix together the pepper, salt, rosemary, basil, oregano, and parsley together in a small bowl.

3. Add the chicken on one of the baking sheets. Sprinkle half of the seasoning mixture on the chicken.

4. Mix together the garlic, bell pepper, onion, and mushrooms in a large bowl. Drizzle the veggies with some oil and toss everything to coast. Spread the veggies on the other baking sheet.

5. Slide these into the oven and allow them to bake for 30 minutes. Stir the vegetables. If the chicken reaches 165 after 30 minutes, remove and cover to keep warm. If it is not cooked through, continue to roast it until it is done.

6. Add the asparagus, balsamic vinegar, olives, tomatoes, and beans, as well as the remaining herb mixture to the tray with the vegetables. Mix everything together.

7. Let the vegetables roast for another 15 minutes or until the asparagus has become crisp-tender.

8. To serve, dice the chicken into bite size pieces and mix into the roasted vegetables.

Shrimp Piccata with Zoodles

Four servings

What You Will Need:

Chopped parsley, 2 tbsp

Rinsed capers, 3 tbsp

Lemon juice, .25 c

White wine, .33 c

Cornstarch, 1 tbsp

Low-sodium chicken broth, 1 c

Peeled and deveined shrimp, 1 lb

Minced garlic, 2 cloves

EVOO, 2 tbsp – divided

Butter, 2 tbsp

Salt, .5 tsp

Trimmed medium zucchinis, 5-6

What You Do:

1. Using a vegetable peeler or a spiralizer, cut the zucchini into noodles. Stop once you reach the seeds of the zucchini. The seeds will cause the noodles to fall apart. Place your noodles in a colander and toss them with some salt. Allow them to drain for 15 to 30 minutes, then gently squeeze them to get rid of excess water.

2. Meanwhile, add the butter and a tablespoon of oil to a large skillet on medium-high. Add in the garlic and allow it to cook for 30 seconds. Add in the shrimp, stirring, for about a minute.

3. Whisk together the cornstarch and broth in a small bowl. Add this to the shrimp along with the wine, capers, and lemon juice.

4. Let this simmer, stirring occasionally, until the shrimp has almost cooked all the way through, about four to five minutes. Take this off the heat.

5. Add the remaining oil to a large skillet and heat. Add the noodles and toss them until they are hot around three minutes. Serve the shrimp and sauce over the noodles with some parsley.

Desserts

Evoo Cake

Eight servings

What You Will Need:

Eggs, 3

Milk, .25 c

Sugar, 1 c

Flour, 1.5 c

Baking powder, 2 tsp

Olive oil, .75 c

Salt

What You Do:

1. Place your oven on 350 and grease a cake pan.

2. Mix together a half a teaspoon of salt, flour, and baking powder together.

3. Whisk together the sugar and eggs, then slowly add in the olive oil and milk.

4. Whisk together the dry and wet ingredients, add to the greased pan, and allow it to bake for 40 minutes. Slice into eight servings and enjoy.

Figs and Cheese

Two servings

What You Will Need:

Honey, 1.5 tsp

Chopped rosemary, 1 sprig

Blue cheese, 2 tbsp

Fresh figs, 3

What You Do:

1. Halve the figs.

2. Spread the cheese over each half of the figs and top with the fresh rosemary. Add some honey to taste.

Avocado and Blueberry Bang

Two servings

What You Will Need:

Maple syrup

Berries, 2 c

Quartered avocado, 2

Frozen banana

What You Do:

1. Place all of the ingredients, except for the syrup in a blender and mix until well combined. Add some ice water if you need to thin the smoothie out.

2. Garnish the smoothie with some syrup.

Date Truffles

10 servings

What You Will Need:

Ground cinnamon, 1 tsp

Orange zest, .75 tsp

Shredded coconut, .5 c

Brewed coffee, 12 oz

Chopped Medjool dates, 3 c

Cocoa powder, .5 c

What You Do:

1. Place the dates in warm coffee. Allow them to soak for five minutes.

2. Take the dates out of the coffee and mash them up into a smooth mixture.

3. Mix in the remaining ingredients, minus the cocoa powder.

4. Form this mixture into small balls. Roll the truffles in cocoa powder.

Chocolate Mousse

Six servings

What You Will Need:

Pinch of salt

Sugar, .5 c divided

Eggs yolks, 7

Orange liqueur, 3 tbsp

Olive oil, .66 c

Melted dark chocolate, 9.5 oz

Orange zest

What You Do:

1. Combine the liqueur, olive oil, and chocolate in a bowl.

2. Whisk the egg yolks together with half of the sugar. Stir it into the chocolate mixture until it becomes smooth.

3. Mix in the salt and remaining sugar.

4. Separate into individual servings. Refrigerate the mixture for 20 minutes before serving.

Banana Strawberry Smoothie

Two servings

What You Will Need:

Skim milk, 1.25 c

Fat-free yogurt, 1.25 c

Orange juice, 2 tbsp

Banana

Sliced strawberries, .75 c

Rolled oats, 4 tbsp

Flaxseed oil, 1 tbsp

Cubed ice, .25 c

What You Do:

1. Place all of the ingredients in a blender and mix until smooth.

Dried Figs with Walnuts and Ricotta

Four servings

What You Will Need:

Honey, 1 tbsp

Halved walnut, 16

Ricotta cheese, .25 c

Halved and dried figs, 8

What You Do:

1. Add the walnuts to a skillet and toast for two minutes.

2. Top the dried figs with the walnuts and cheese.

3. Drizzle them with honey and serve.

Summer Fruit Granita

Four servings

What You Will Need:

Raspberries, .5 c

Lemon juice, 2 tbsp

Orange juice, .25 c

Water, .5 c

Sugar, .5 c

Ripe nectarines, 1 lb

What You Do:

1. Boil the nectarines with the sugar for ten minutes.

2. Mix in the raspberries.

3. Add in the juices and extra sugar you feel that it needs it.

4. Place the mixture in a freezer safe bowl and freeze for 30 minutes. Use a fork to stir the ice crystals to form the granite.

Strawberry and Ricotta Parfait

Six servings

What You Will Need:

Lemon zest, .25 tsp

Light agave nectar, 3 tbsp

Ricotta cheese, 15 oz

Sugar, 1 tsp

Mint, 1 tbsp

Strawberries, 1 lb

Fresh mint

Vanilla, .5 tsp

What You Do:

1. Gently stir together the mint, sugar, and berries. Allow this to rest for at least ten minutes.

2. In another bowl, stir together the vanilla, lemon zest, ricotta, and agave nectar. Use an electric mixer to combine everything for about two minutes on medium speed.

3. To make the parfaits – place a tablespoon of the ricotta mixture in the bottom of six glasses. Top with part of the strawberry mixture. Repeat these two layers and garnish it with some mint.

4. These can be chilled for up to four hours before serving or you can serve immediately.

Honey Pistachio Pears

Six servings

What You Will Need:

Powdered sugar, 2 tbsp

Orange zest, 1 tsp

Pear nectar, .25 c

Honey, 3 tbsp

Butter, 2 tbsp

Medium pears, 3

Salted pistachios, .33 c

Mascarpone cheese, .5 c

What You Do:

1. Start by placing your oven to 400.

2. Peel, core, and slice the pears in half. Place them cut side down in a baking dish.

3. Mix together the zest, butter, honey, and nectar. Pour the mixture over the pears. Roast the pears, uncovered, for 20 to 25 minutes.

4. As the pears bake, spoon the juices over them occasionally until they are tcndcr.

Chia Seed Pumpkin Pudding

Four servings

What You Will Need:

Chia seeds, .5 c

Almond milk, 1.25 c

Pumpkin puree, 1 c

Pumpkin spice, 2 tsp

Maple syrup, .25 c

What You Do:

1. For the best results, add all of the ingredients into a jar and allow it to sit overnight. If you don't have overnight, at least let it sit for 15 minutes.

2. Once you are ready to eat, top it with a quarter of a cup of fresh blueberries, some sliced almonds, and some sunflower seeds.

Halva

Four servings

What You Will Need:

EVOO, 1 c

Water, 4 c

Honey, 1 c

Cloves, 3

Ground cinnamon, 1 tbsp

Cinnamon sticks, 3

Sugar, 3 c

Sliced almonds, 1 c

Uncooked semolina, 1 c

What You Do:

1. Place the water in a pot, along with the sugar, cloves, and cinnamon sticks. Allow this to boil gently for five minutes. Remove the pot from the heat and remove the cinnamon sticks and cloves. Stir in the honey and set to the side.

2. In another pan, heat the oil and add in the semolina. Stir constantly until the mixture had become golden brown. Add in a half of a teaspoon of cinnamon.

3. Slowly pour simple syrup you made earlier into the semolina mixture. Keep the heat on, and constantly stir until it thickens. Mix in the almonds. Once everything is combined, pour into a domed glass bowl and allow it to cool.

4. Flip the Halva out on a plate and sprinkle with the rest of the cinnamon.

Roasted Figs and Spicy Mascarpone

Four servings

What You Will Need:

Orange juice, 2 tbsp

Ginger root syrup, 1 tbsp

Ground cinnamon, 2 tsp

Dice up some ginger

Mascarpone, 4 oz

Sugar, 2 tbsp

Clear honey, 2 tbsp

Butter, 2 tbsp

Halved and trimmed figs, 8

What You Do:

1. Place your oven to 400.

2. Lay the figs out on a baking sheet and place a small bit of butter on each one. Drizzle them with honey and top with cinnamon, orange juice, and sugar.

3. Allow these to bake for 15 minutes.

4. Add the ginger and syrup to the mascarpone and mix together.

5. Top each of the figs with the mascarpone mixture and serve while warm.

Greek Parfait

Two servings

What You Will Need:

Orange juice, 1 tsp

Pomegranate seeds, 2-3 oz

Chopped pistachios, 2-3 oz

Cubed mango

Greek yogurt, 12 oz

What You Do:

1. Mix the yogurt and orange juice together.

2. Divide the mango between two separate dessert bowls. Cover the fruit with a layer of yogurt mixture. Sprinkle the top with pistachios. Cover the nuts with the rest of the yogurt and garnish with the pomegranate.

3. Chill the parfait in the fridge until you are ready to enjoy.

Italian Apple Olive Oil Cake

Eight servings

What You Will Need:

Gold raisins, .66 c

Eggs, 2

EVOO, 1 c

Sugar, 1 c

Baking soda, 1 tsp

Baking powder, 1 tsp

Ground nutmeg, .5 tsp

Ground cinnamon, .5 tsp

All-purpose flour, 3 c

Orange juice

Chopped and peeled Gala apples, 2 large

What You Do:

1. Soak the raisins in warm water for 15 minutes and drain them well.

2. Place your oven to 350.

3. Put the chopped apples in a bowl and pour in some orange juice. Add just enough juice to be able to toss and coat the apples so that they don't brown.

4. In a large bowl, sift the baking soda, baking powder, nutmeg, cinnamon, and flour together. Set this to the side.

5. In a stand mixer with a whisk attachment, add in the olive oil and sugar. Mix on low for about two minutes, or until well combined.

6. With the mixer still on, add in the eggs, one at a time. Let this mix for two minutes until the mixture has grown in volume. It needs to be thicker, but still on the runny side.

7. In the bowl with the dry ingredients, form a well in the middle. Add in the wet ingredients. With a wooden spoon, mix everything together until it had just come together. This is going to be a thick batter. You do not need to loosen it.

8. Drain the raisins that have been soaking and drain the apples of any excess juice. Add the apples and raisins to the batter and mix it together until well combined. The batter should still be thick.

9. Line a nine-inch cake pan with parchment. Spoon the batter into the pan and level it off with a spoon.

10. Bake this for 45 minutes at 350. A toothpick inserted in the center should come out clean.

11. Allow this pan to cool completely. Once you are ready, lift the parchment up to move the cake over to a serving dish. Dust the top with some powdered sugar.

12. You could also heat some dark honey to serve on top.

Chocolate Chip Cookies

24 servings

What You Will Need:

Semisweet chocolate chips, 2 c

Baking soda, .5 tsp

All-purpose flour, 2 c

Egg

Salt, 1 tsp

Golden brown sugar, .75 c

Sugar, .75 c

Vanilla, 1 tbsp

EVOO, 1 c

What You Do:

1. Start by placing your oven to 350. Place parchment on two cookie sheets and set aside.

2. Place a teaspoon of salt, both sugars, vanilla, and olive oil in a large mixing bowl. Mix together until it forms a smooth consistency.

3. Mix in the egg, blending until it is smooth.

4. Add the baking soda and flour to the bowl and combine until it is completely incorporated and you can't see any blobs of flour.

5. Fold the chocolate chips into the batter.

6. With your hands, form the batter into two tablespoons sized balls. Place the balls on the cookie sheets. Try to keep about two inches between the cookies.

7. Flatten the cookies just slightly with the palm of your hand.

8. Sprinkle the tops with some salt.

9. Place in the oven and allow it to cook for about ten to 12 minutes. The edges should be golden brown. Allow the cookies to cool on the cookie sheet for around five minutes. Place them on a cooling rack to come to room temp.

Brownies

12 servings

What You Will Need:

Chopped walnuts, .33 c

Salt, .25 tsp

Baking powder, .25 tsp

Cocoa powder, .33 c

Flour, .5 c

Eggs, 2

Vanilla, 1 tsp

Sugar, .75 c

Greek yogurt, .25 c

Olive oil, .25 c

What You Do:

1. Start by placing your oven to 350.

2. Mix together the sugar and olive oil until they become smooth. Mix in the vanilla.

3. Beat the eggs together in a small bowl and then stir into the olive oil mixture.

4. Blend in the yogurt.

5. In a separate bowl, mix together the baking powder, salt, cocoa powder, and flour. Add this to the olive oil mixture. Stir until everything is well mixed.

6. Stir in the nuts.

7. Place parchment part in a 9-inch square baking pan and pour in the brownie mixture. Smooth the top out with a spatula.

8. Allow this to bake for 25 minutes.

9. Allow the brownies to cool and then remove from the pan from pulling the parchment. Cut into squares.

Greek Yogurt Chocolate Mousse

Four servings

What You Will Need:

Vanilla, .5 tsp

Honey, 1 tbsp

Greek yogurt, 2 c

Dark chocolate, 3.5 oz

Milk, .75 c

What You Do:

1. Place the chocolate and the milk in a pot. Gently heat the milk until the chocolate melts. Make sure that you don't let this boil. Once the chocolate and the milk have combined, add in the vanilla and the honey and stir together.

2. Spoon the Greek yogurt into a large bowl and pour the chocolate over it. Mix everything together and then spoon the mixture into four individual serve bowls or glasses.

3. Chill this for at least two hours. Serve the mouse topped with some Greek yogurt and fresh raspberries.

4. This will keep in the fridge for two days.

Turkish Yogurt Cake with Figs

Eight servings

What You Will Need:

Halved figs, 4 to 6

Butter

Orange blossom water, 1.5 tsp

Juice and zest of ½ of a lemon

Greek yogurt, 1.5 c

Sifted all-purpose flour, 3 tbsp

Sugar, .5 c

Separated eggs, 4

What You Do:

1. Start by placing your oven to 375.

2. Beat the egg yolks and the sugar until they are light and creamy. Add in the flour and mix together until combined. Stir in the orange blossom water, lemon juice and zest, and yogurt.

3. Beat the egg whites with an egg beater until they form a stiff peak. Gently fold this into the batter until combined.

4. Grease a 9-inch springform pan with the butter. Pour the batter in and arrange the figs over the top, face up.

5. Let the cake bake for 50 minutes or until the top has turned golden brown and is springy.

6. The cake rises a lot, but it will decrease once taken from the oven.

7. Allow this to cool completely and then dust it with powdered sugar.

Snacks

Calamari Rings

Four servings

What You Will Need:

Pepper

Salt

EVOO, for frying

Dried oregano, .5 tbsp

Paprika, .5 tbsp

Semolina flour, 1.5 oz

Bread flour, 3.5 oz

Sliced calamari, 25 oz

What You Do:

1. Clean the calamari slices and pat them dry with paper towels.

2. Add the pepper, salt, oregano, paprika, and both flours to a bowl and mix them together.

3. Coat the calamari in the mixture, making sure that it is completely covered.

4. Fry the calamari in the EVOO. Make sure the oil is heated so that it sizzles when water is dripped in, otherwise the calamari will soak up the oil and be greasy.

5. Drain on a paper towel and serve with a squeeze of lemon.

Peanut Butter Popcorn

Four servings

What You Will Need:

Agave syrup, .25 c

Peanut butter, .33 c

Chopped peanuts, .33 c

Sea salt, .5 tsp

Popcorn kernel, .5 c

Peanut oil, 2 tbsp

Wildflower honey, .25 c

What You Do:

1. Add the peanut oil and popcorn kernels to a pot.

2. Over medium heat, shake the pot slowly until all of the corn has popped.

3. In another pot, mix together the agave syrup and honey. Cook this over low heat for about five minutes and then mix in the peanut butter.

4. Pour this over the popped popcorn and toss to coat.

Parmesan Herbed Walnuts

Eight servings

What You Will Need:

Egg white

Walnuts, 2 c

Garlic salt, .5 tsp

Parsley flakes, 1 tsp

Italian herb seasoning, .5 tsp

Parmigiano-Reggiano cheese, .5 c

Cayenne

What You Do:

1. Place your oven on 250.

2. Combine all of the ingredients together except for the egg whites and walnuts.

3. Whisk the egg whites together and stir in the halved walnuts.

4. Mix together the cheese mixture and the walnuts.

5. Place on a baking sheet that has been greased and bake for 30 minutes. Serve the walnuts cold.

Eggplant Crunchy Bites

Four servings

What You Will Need:

Pepper

Salt

EVOO

All-purpose flour, 7 oz

Light beer, 12 oz

Sliced eggplants, 2

What You Do:

1. Lay the sliced eggplants out flat and sprinkle them with salt on both sides. Place them on some paper towels. This will remove excess water. After they have set for 30 minutes, brush the salt off of them and pat them dry.

2. To a bowl, add the beer and sift in the flowers. Stir as you go so that you can get rid of lumps. Add in pepper and salt to taste. The batter should be a thick creamy consistency. It shouldn't be too runny. Allow this to chill for 30 minutes.

3. Once the batter has set, dip the eggplant slices in the batter, making sure that they are completely coated.

4. Add the EVOO to a skillet and allow to heat up. Place the eggplant slices in and allow them to fry for a couple of minutes on both sides. Lay them on some paper towels to drain.

Pita Pizza

Eight servings

What You Will Need:

Pepper

Salt

Green salad leaves, 1 c

Pesto, 2 tsp

Dried oregano, .5 tsp

Tomato paste, 4 tbsp

Sliced large tomato

Grated mozzarella, 14 oz

Pitas, 4

What You Do:

1. Place your oven on 250.

2. Lay the pitas on a baking sheet and spread them each with a tablespoon of tomato paste. Sprinkle them with some pepper, salt, and oregano.

3. Then spread them each with a half of a teaspoon of pesto. Sprinkle them with mozzarella, add sliced tomato, and sprinkle with more mozzarella.

4. Slide this into the oven for ten minutes or until the cheese has melted.

5. Allow these to cool a bit and then cut them in half.

6. Serve them with a small green salad.

Feta Triangle

Eight servings

What You Will Need:

Pepper

EVOO, 1 tbsp

Milk, 1 tbsp

Chopped dill, .25 c

Egg

Parmesan, 2 oz

Grated gouda, 2 oz

Crumbled feta, 6 oz

Filo pastry, 8 sheets

What You Do:

1. Start by placing the oven to 3250.

2. Crush up the feta cheese with the back of the spoon in a large bowl. Mix in the pepper, dill, milk, egg, and gouda. Make sure everything is mixed well.

3. Lay out a sheet of filo and brush with some oil. Top with another sheet, again, brushing with some oil. Slice this into four squares and place a tablespoon of cheese filling at a corner on each of the filo squares. Bring the opposite corner over the cheese filling to form a triangle and cover the filling.

4. Repeat this process for the rest of the filo sheets. You should 16 triangles in total.

5. Oil a baking sheet and lay the triangles on it. Brush them with some oil.

6. Bake the triangles for 20 to 25 minutes.

7. These can be served warm or cold.

Halloumi Sticks

Eight servings

What You Will Need:

Pepper

EVOO, .5 tbsp

Lemon juice 2 tsp

Dried oregano, .25 tsp

Halloumi cheese, 6 oz

What You Do:

1. Slice the halloumi cheese into sticks that are three to four inches long and a half-inch thick.

2. Add the oil to a skillet and allow it to heat up.

3. Roll the cheese in the dried oregano and place in the oil to fry. Cook on both sides for one to two minutes.

4. Place them on a small plate and sprinkle with some pepper and lemon juice.

Feta Dip

Eight servings

What You Will Need:

Lemon juice, 1 tsp

Cayenne pepper, 1 tsp

Chopped pre-roasted bell peppers, 4 oz

Pre-cooked hot chili peppers, 2 oz

Ricotta cheese, 8 oz

Crumbled feta, 8 oz

What You Do:

1. Add the cayenne, bell peppers, and chili to a food processor and mix until it forms a smooth paste. Stir in the crumbled feta.

2. In another bowl, stir together the lemon juice and ricotta. Add this to the feta mixture and stir until well combined.

3. Chill before serving.

Cinnamon Couscous

Four servings

What You Will Need:

Pepper

Salt

EVOO, 1 tbsp

Orange juice, 2 tbsp

Chicken broth, 2 c

Dried cilantro, 1 tsp

Cinnamon, tsp

Raisins, .33 c

Whole-wheat couscous, 10 oz

What You Do:

1. Pour the broth in a pot and allow it to come to a boil.

2. Add in the pepper, salt, and oil. Take off the heat and stir in the cilantro, raisins, and couscous.

3. Allow this to stand for five minutes.

4. Stir in the orange juice and cinnamon. Fluff with a fork and serve.

Panzanella

Nine servings

What You Will Need:

Pepper

Salt

EVOO, 3 tbsp

Lemon juice, 4 tbsp

Chopped oregano, 2 tbsp

Pitted olives, 1 c

Sliced small red onion

Chopped tomatoes, 3 lb

Crumbled feta, 6 oz

Artisan bread loaf cubes, 10 c

What You Do:

1. The day before you plan on serving, lay the bread pieces out on a baking sheet so that it hardens up overnight. Or, you can bake it at 300 for about 15 minutes.

2. Place the onions in a bowl of cold water and let them soak for ten minutes. Drain.

3. Mix together the olives and the tomatoes.

4. To make the dressing, whisk together the pepper, salt, oregano, lemon juice, and oil.

5. Mix the onions in with the olive mixture. Add in the bread pieces and then pour in the marinade. Stir everything together. Allow this to stand for no longer than four hours. Stir the mixture occasionally to make sure that the lemon juice covers everything.

6. Stir in the feta before you serve.

Crunchy Chickpeas

Four servings

What You Will Need:

Salt

EVOO, 2 tbsp

Turmeric, .5 tsp

Chili powder, .5 tsp

Cumin, 1 tsp

Curry powder, 1 tsp

Drained and rinsed chickpeas, 2 15-oz cans

What You Do:

1. Make sure that your chickpeas are completely dried and any loose skins are removed.

2. Place the chickpeas in a bowl and add in the salt and oil. Stir everything together until the chickpeas are completely covered. Put them in a 400-degree oven for 30 minutes. Turn them every ten minutes. Don't be concerned if they pop.

3. Combine all of the spices and some salt together.

4. As soon as the chickpeas are crispy, sprinkle them with the spice mixture.

5. They should be served warm so that they stay crispy.

Hummus

Four servings

What You Will Need:

Salt

EVOO, 1 tbsp

Water, 4 tbsp

Lemon juice, 2 tbsp

Cumin, 1 tsp

Paprika, 1 tsp

Tahini, 1 tbsp

Chickpeas, 7 oz

Crushed garlic, 2 cloves

What You Do:

1. Rinse and drain the chickpeas.

2. Using a food processor add in the tahini, cumin, garlic, water, lemon juice, and olive oil. Blend everything together until it forms a smooth puree.

3. Add the chickpeas and blend until smooth.

4. Serve with a sprinkle of paprika and some quartered pita bread.

Pita Chips

Four servings

What You Will Need:

EVOO, 2 tbsp

Whole-wheat pita bread, 2 large

What You Do:

1. Slice the pita bread into 16 portions.

2. Spread them out on a baking sheet and brush them with some olive oil.

3. Place them in a 350-degree oven and let them bake for six minutes on both sides.

4. Use some extra oil if you need to.

Greek Nachos

Four servings

What You Will Need:

Lemon juice, 1 tbsp

Oregano, 1 tbsp

EVOO, 2 tbsp

Pepper

Shredded lettuce, 1 c

Sliced olives, 2 tbsp

Crumbled feta, .25 c

Quartered cherry tomatoes, .5 c

Chopped white onion, 2 tbsp

Hummus, .33 c

Pita chips, 3 c

What You Do:

1. Whisk together the pepper, oregano, lemon juice, and oil. Stir this into the hummus.

2. Spread the pita chips across a large serving platter and distribute the majority of the hummus over the top. Make sure you save some for later.

3. Cover this with feta, olives, tomatoes, onions, and lettuce. Top with the remaining hummus mixture and enjoy.

Trail Mix

Servings vary

What You Will Need:

Dark chocolate chips, .5 to .66 c

Dried banana slices or unsweetened banana chips, 6 oz

Vanilla, 1 tsp

Coconut oil, 2 to 3 tbsp

Coconut sugar, .33 c

Unsweetened coconut flakes, 1 c

Raw cashew halves, 1 c

Raw walnut halves, 2 c

What You Do:

1. Place the coconut oil, vanilla, sugar, coconut, and nuts in a crock pot. Mix everything together and set to high to cook for 45 to 60 minutes. Stir the mixture a few times to check and make sure that the coconut flakes don't burn. After 45 minutes, if the flakes look like they are burning, turn the heat to low.

2. Turn the heat to low for the next 20 to 30 minutes.

3. Take out the trails mix onto a piece of parchment paper to let it dry out. Make sure that you allow it to cool for at least 15 minutes before you add in the banana and chocolate.

4. Mix in the chocolate chips and banana chips.

5. Keep this stored in a Ziplock bag or in an airtight container.

Smoked Salmon Bites

Four servings

What You Will Need:

Smoked salmon, 1 pack

Herbed goat cheese, 1 pack

Endive, 3 heads

What You Do:

1. Cut the ends off of the endive and pull the leaves apart.

2. Spread the goat cheese on the inside of the endive leaves.

3. Lay a salmon slice on top of the goat cheese. Enjoy.

Conclusion

Thanks for making it through to the end of *Mediterranean Diet for Beginners*. I hope it was informative and able to provide you with all of the information you need to achieve your goals whatever they may be.

You now have all the tools to help you start a Mediterranean diet. Head to the grocery store and stock up on the essentials, and get going on your 14-day meal plan. You will be amazed at how easy it is to follow once you get started. Don't continue to put things off until the "time is right." The time is right now, so get started.

Finally, if you found this book useful in any way, a review on Amazon is always appreciated!

Printed in Poland
by Amazon Fulfillment
Poland Sp. z o.o., Wrocław